MOANA HOTEL

OUTRIGGER
CANOE CLUB

Photo taken in 1923

HUSTACE
RESIDENCE

MOANA HOTEL
PIER

OANA HOTEL

STEINER
RESIDENCE

PRINCE KUHIO
RESIDENCE

WAIKIKI
TAVERN

Photo taken in 1923

HAWAIIAN YESTERDAYS

Historical Photographs by Ray Jerome Baker

Adele Robinson (Mrs. Herman Lemke), Old Plantation, 1910

HAWAIIAN YESTERDAYS

Historical Photographs by
Ray Jerome Baker

Edited by Robert E. Van Dyke—Text by Ronn Ronck

Mutual Publishing Company
Honolulu

A NOTE ABOUT THE PHOTOGRAPHS

Ray Jerome Baker took thousands of pictures of Hawaii during his lifetime. In selecting those which appear in this book a number of factors were considered.

These include historical significance, artistic quality and subject matter. Some of the photographs, too, were chosen for the book simply because they were among Baker's favorites.

In organizing the book we wanted to capture the spirit of Baker's work and the old Hawaii that he loved so much. Any one of the individual sections could have been developed into a book of its own.

The color photographs were reproduced from lantern slides hand-tinted by Baker's wife, Edith, and other studio employees. While some are of lesser quality than others, they all give us a historical perspective to Baker's world and contribute to our understanding of his attempts to produce color photographs before their time.

First Printing Sept. 1982
Second Printing Nov. 1982
Third Printing Feb. 1983
Fourth Printing Sept. 1983

Library of Congress Card Catalogue Number 82-81505

International Standard Book Number 0-935180-03-6

Mutual Publishing Company
2055 North King Street
Honolulu, Hawaii 96819
U.S.A.

Printed in Japan

A REMINISCENCE AND AN APPRECIATION OF RAY JEROME BAKER

It is both difficult and easy to think back and write about Ray Jerome Baker. Easy because there was so much about the man to admire, respect and love; difficult because his friendship meant so much to me.

Our acquaintance began when I was less than a day old and he escorted my grandmother into the hospital to visit me. There, amid the consternation of the nurses, he tried to use his archaic and appearingly dirty camera to take my photograph. Unfortunately, the nurses would not let him do so and I never came to know how I looked during that first important day of my life.

It is said in our family that it was love at first sight. I cannot vouch for Baker but, as for myself, there can be no doubt in a relationship that lasted for a full 35 years.

I always looked in awe at my grandmother and Baker for they had both been born in December, 1880—he on the first day and she on the 21st day. They were both good and kindly people who gave generously to anyone and everyone.

Their greatest bond was a mutual love of Hawaii and for all things Hawaiian. Their greatest opposites and extremes were political. He was a Socialist and she was of the Republican persuasion, a fact he never thoroughly understood.

They met shortly after his arrival in 1910 when he rented a house along the Beach Road, now Ala Moana Boulevard, at a location today occupied by part of Kaiser Hospital. Over the years he came to photograph our family on many important and significant occasions.

He was there to photograph my mother at 12 in her ballet costume and at the age of 18 in 1926 when she took hula lessons from Louise Beamer. He was not present to photograph my parents during their wedding ceremony in 1934 but he came to the luau that afternoon and to the hospital the day I was born three years later.

My earliest real recollections of Ray Jerome Baker go back to 1941, my third, going on fourth year. He had come to photograph at Punahou during one of the school's centennial pageants.

Throughout my years of growing up my biggest thrill was visiting Baker's studio. Sundays were set aside, not for church since Baker did not believe in that, but for relaxation or perhaps a trip into the country. He was planning such a trip that Sunday morning of Dec. 7, 1941 when the Japanese planes attacked Pearl Harbor.

During the war my father often took me to Baker's studio and here I learned the delights and mysteries of the photographer's art. As I stood at his side in the darkroom I would look around at the hand-blown bottles full of chemicals and listen to the constantly running water. Here, too, glowed a red light that was far different from the blackout bulbs that burned in our household.

I was barely able to see over his sink and into the large glass trays. Before my eyes blank pieces of paper turned into photographs of nameless individuals and unknown buildings.

Baker obeyed the military authorities during

Emma D. Richey, 1947   Gladys Richey, 1920   Gladys Richey, 1926

World War II and did not photograph any subject, such as landscapes or city scenes, that could have benefited the enemy. Instead, like most of the other civilian photographers in Honolulu, he made his living taking portraits of servicemen stationed in Hawaii or those passing through on their way overseas.

After the war came to an end, Baker once again took his cameras outdoors but he would only have another 15 years left of active photography. He was now more interested in cataloging his extensive collection of pictures and publishing them in limited-edition books.

When my father died in June of 1951, just past his fortieth birthday, I began to make even more frequent visits to the Baker studio. One day, in early 1953, I dropped by after school. He was sitting among stacks of glass plate negatives, many of which measured 11 x 14 in size.

The Bishop Museum, which was to get much of his collection, was not interested at that time in storing negatives larger than 5 x 7. He asked me if I would like them and they became the nucleus of my current Baker photo collection, many of which appear in this book. Previous to this he had presented me with cameras, records, letters and other personal effects.

Shortly after giving me these large-format negatives, Baker took me into an area of his studio that I had never seen before. The door was locked and the dark room was musty and hung heavy with cobwebs. Here had been his motion picture studio and the room still contained washing and drying vats. Against one wall were the cans containing his old motion

picture films and he told me that I could have them all.

Baker drove me home that afternoon in his second-hand, war-time Jeep. The vehicle was loaded to the seams with the motion picture cans. I remember that when we rounded the corner at McCully and Beretania streets several of the cans rolled out and clanked down the road. We gave a merry chase, captured each of them and once again continued on our way.

Baker, as I well recall, neither smoked nor drank and yet was unoffended by those who did. His favorite food was a pot roast, heavy with vegetables, which he cooked once a week by himself. He liked milk and iced tea, tuna fish sandwiches and ice cream.

He was a man of very modest taste. Never stingy with a dime but not wasteful either. He slept on a simple couch and took a cold water bath twice a day.

Dress was an easy matter. He always wore a long-sleeved shirt and often a bow tie. I once bought him a very simple and conservative "aloha shirt" but he apologized and gave it away to the yard boy.

His suits were always mail-ordered by catalogue from Sears Roebuck and Co., in Chicago. Neither his size nor the style ever varied. The only sure gift, something he was bound to need and appreciate, was a new tie.

In photography his fulfillment came in a happy smiling face, the never-ending supply of beautiful scenes in these Islands, a rainbow, a full swell in a wave at the beach at Waikiki and clouds that floated overhead. He was a man

Gladys and Roy Van Dyke at their wedding reception, 1934

Gladys and Robert Van Dyke on a hike with Baker, 1942

Robert E. Van Dyke, the last photo Baker took at his 1911 Kalakaua Avenue studio, 1959.

constantly excited by the world around him.

During 1960, I encouraged Baker to revisit many of the spots he had photographed in 1910 when he had decided to become a permanent resident. I wanted him to make a retrospect collection 50 years later.

By then, of course, his old camera was frequently out of focus. I found much satisfaction in hopping under the black cloth after he had finished and correcting his adjustments before the picture was snapped. My concern would save him embarrassment later in the darkroom.

I remember our trip together to Kauai and the great kindness of Grace Buscher at Coco Palms who was overjoyed to have him on the premises of her hotel. He had reached an age and reputation where he was truly one of the most famous men in Hawaii and yet he did not completely realize it. Everywhere we went there were turning heads and silent smiles of respected admiration. "Why there is Mr. Baker, the famous photographer," some would say.

He never heard most of these comments, however, because he was incredibly hard of hearing. I learned to communicate by looking directly at him when we talked.

Baker loved children and could get them to smile as quick as a wink. He would say to a little girl, "why you are beautiful, how many children do you have?"

The girl would laugh and remind him that she was only a child herself. "Oh, I thought you were a menehune," he replied and took the picture.

You could go nowhere with Baker without him informing you about the proper names of plants, fish and geology. He was a man of more than normal curiosity, well-read beyond his time. His interests had no limit, his knowledge no end.

He experimented with time-lapse photography long before most people dared to imagine its possibilities and was photographing through a microscope as early as 1912. Some of his motion picture techniques were still considered unusual in 1977 when I began publicly showing, once again, the priceless film that he had shot between 1910 and 1935. I am sure Baker would have been proud of the popularity of his films which helped raise close to $190,000 for public charities.

Baker was, by every definition, a true Renaissance man. In his prime he was aware of everything about him, participating, creating and recreating. He was a pioneer in many fields of science and art.

He deeply loved everything about Hawaii and realized early that his calling was to document change in the Islands. Few of the things he photographed have remained the same. People have gone, beautiful scenes have vanished and buildings have come down.

When Ray Jerome Baker died in 1972, I lost a dear friend and Hawaii lost one of its finest artists. I feel privileged to have known him and take pride in being able to share with the readers of this book a small part of the great legacy he left behind for us to enjoy.

—*Robert E. Van Dyke*

Preface

Although he died in 1972, just a month shy of his 92nd birthday, it is still impossible to escape the presence of Ray Jerome Baker. He was Hawaii's premier photographer during the first half of the 20th century and through the greatness of his art he has shaped our vision of that period in island history.

It is rare to find a person today who has not seen a Baker photograph. His work was published widely during his lifetime and he gave frequent lectures that were illustrated with his slides and motion pictures.

He also printed photographs for a number of limited-edition books which he produced and sold himself. One of these was called *Hawaiian Yesterdays,* and its title has been borrowed for the present volume which is being published on the 10th anniversary year of his death.

With an eye toward history, Baker laid the foundation for his own biography. He kept accurate records of his activities in Hawaii and published accounts of his major travels abroad. He kept carbon copies of his letters and each year bound them for reference.

Baker compiled an ancestral history of his family in the late 1940's and, in 1964, published his own autobiography, *Odyssey of a Cameraman.* The latter was 153 pages long and contained numerous photographs. He printed about 250 copies and distributed them to his friends.

The person primarily responsible for the present-day interest in Baker's life and work is Robert E. Van Dyke, a noted collector of Hawaiiana and the editor of this book. Baker was a long-time friend of the Van Dyke family and over the years he gave Robert, and his mother, Gladys R. Van Dyke, the photographs reproduced in this edition of "Hawaiian Yesterdays."

Books such as this one do not appear out of thin air. Most take months, if not years, of hard work. They are also essentially group endeavors.

Hawaiian Yesterdays, of course, would not have been possible without Robert E. Van Dyke and his mother, Gladys R. Van Dyke. Their personal collection of Ray Jerome Baker photographs and other material make up the heart of this book. Mr. Van Dyke chose the photographs, provided caption information and helped edit the text.

Rubin Young designed *Hawaiian Yesterdays,* from front to back. His skills in layout, typography, and printing were essential ingredients as the book grew from concept to reality. Everyone involved with the project benefited from his knowledge and experience.

Norman Shapiro copied hundreds of Baker's lantern slides and prints. His excellent photographic work saved countless hours during the final selection of pictures for this book.

Lynn Davis, curator of photography at the Bernice P. Bishop Museum, has provided the Introduction to this volume. Her help and advice during the research stages of the project is also greatly appreciated.

Finally, a special acknowledgment is due to Bennett Hymer who has produced and published *Hawaiian Yesterdays.* Without his long-term support and enthusiasm this book would not have been possible. He has been a true collaborator in every sense of the word.

—Ronn Ronck

Introduction

When Ray Jerome Baker came to Hawai'i in 1908, his initial response to the picturesque beauty of the islands and a persisting Polynesian ambience was largely a romantic one. His desire was to photograph Hawai'i and its people "for whatever aesthetic interest they might have," and his early images reflect a sharp sense of the idyllic.

The growing lure of Hawai'i as a tourist mecca in the early 1900s increased opportunities for photographers. Baker found a ready market for his images in *Paradise of the Pacific*, a magazine begun in the 1890s by another Honolulu photographer, J.J. Williams, to promote tourism. *The Mid-Pacific Magazine*, founded in 1911 by Baker's friend Alexander Hume Ford, relied heavily on photographs. The newly formed Hawaii Promotion Committee also found photography, including motion pictures, a most effective way to sell Hawai'i. Baker contributed heavily to all of these and in the late 1930s began publishing his own books.

As time passed and changes came more quickly to Hawai'i, altering forever the landscape and the culture, Baker became aware that his images embodied something much more important than his own vision. He saw that he had captured the images of a land and a people in transition. For the most part, Baker's predecessors had created popular, contrived studio portraits of native Hawaiians. Although he was by no means the first to take a view camera into the field to photograph Hawaiians, Baker had made this his standard. One of his first books, *Hawaiian Yesterdays*, brought together these early portraits.

Perhaps it was his awareness of the rapidly changing lifestyle of native Hawaiians in the early 20th century that led him to research collections of photographs and illustrations of 19th-century Hawaii. Baker published books of such early images, collected from many sources, and spent years researching locations in Honolulu. *Honolulu Then and Now*, published in 1941, juxtaposed his own images of Honolulu in the 1930s with those of his predecessors. Through such books as this, Baker continued to record the changing beauty of Hawai'i.

In the mid-1950s, at the age of 75, Baker began giving his negatives and prints to Bishop Museum so that his strong vision would be perpetuated and shared with future generations. Today, Bishop Museum is heir to the Baker legacy. When he died in 1972, he endowed the Museum to "perpetually establish and maintain" the Ray Jerome Baker Room "in order that the people may forever remember the beauty of old Hawaii and as an inspiration to the people to help perpetuate the present beauty of Hawaii."

The Ray Jerome Baker Room at Bishop Museum includes a public research facility where the community may discover the large and varied pictorial history of Hawai'i. The Museum's programs also include staff lectures, publishing, exhibitions of works by Hawai'i photographers, and development of traveling exhibitions which carry Baker's vision far beyond the walls of the Museum.

This book of photographs by Baker from the personal collection of Robert E. Van Dyke gives us another opportunity to explore the depth of Baker's gift to the people of Hawai'i.

Lynn Davis, Curator of Photography
Bernice P. Bishop Museum

This volume is dedicated
by
Robert E. Van Dyke
to
Mrs. Gladys R. Van Dyke,
my mother, who made a precious friendship
of thirty-five years a possibility for me
and
to Her Majesty, Helen, Queen Mother
of Roumania, Princess of Greece, Germany,
Denmark and Great Britain, who has never
visited these Islands but will now have
a chance to enjoy some of the Hawaii
that was, of which I have told her,
and
to the memory of
those dear friends that knew and loved
the Hawaii of old,
Emma Lyons Doyle, Lucia and Bert Lyons
and
H.R.H., Edward, Duke of Windsor
who never forgot surfing and riding
the waves at the Moana in 1920
and
last but not least, to my beloved grandmother
Emma D. Richey

TABLE OF CONTENTS

Ray Jerome Baker in Eureka, California. Photograph by Emma Freeman, 1922

"I feel I have been a most fortunate person, for I have had a hobby for my occupation for more than fifty years... I never expected it to make me rich, but it has made me happy..."

R. J. BAKER, PHOTOGRAPHER

Ray Jerome Baker first visited Hawaii at the age of 28. He and his wife of two years, Edith Frost, planned the trip as a delayed two-week honeymoon but they fell in love with the Islands and ended up staying four months.

"My camera on this trip," Baker wrote in *Odyssey of a Cameraman*, his 1964 autobiography, "was made good use of and I carried with me many interesting and some beautiful shots of island scenes. The negatives served me to good purpose in after years, and most of them I still have. California seemed drab and uninviting after the glamour of Hawaii. During the year and a half that followed, we could only be happy by planning to return."

Baker, who would eventually become the most famous photographer in the Islands, was born Dec. 1, 1880 on a farm in Owen Center, eight miles north of Rockford, Illinois. He was the fourth child in the family of three boys and two girls.

When he was a little over a year old, they moved to rural Brownsdale Village, near Austin, in southern Minnesota. It was here that he became interested in the outdoors, natural history and eventually photography.

The farm house of his youth was a true pioneer home, fashioned of split logs and wooden shingles. Inside, the logs were first caulked in-between and later plastered over. There was no electricity and kerosene lamps were used for lighting.

William Baker, his father, raised wheat and corn. His mother, Sarah Palmer Baker, kept food on the table and assumed the major responsibility for raising the five children. When Baker was three or four years old the family was struck by scarlet fever and the illness lingered around the household for six months. Ray was hit the hardest and he contracted an ear infection that remained with him for the rest of his life. In later years he had difficulties with his hearing and this loss turned him into somewhat of a recluse.

At the age of seven, Baker was taken by his mother to Chicago to see an ear specialist. The doctor's treatment helped a little but the trip was probably more important by the fact that Baker was able to visit his first photo studio. He had his portrait taken while sitting on a paper-mache rock and holding a walking stick and straw hat. A hazy backdrop and a rug of artificial grass completed the picture.

"I recall that the photographer," Baker wrote many years later, "after placing me favorably in this rustic scene, stepped back to the big camera and went into hiding. He drew the heavy focusing cloth over his head, corrected the camera's position, and drew my attention as he snapped. It was too early in my life's experienc-

William and Sarah Baker, parents of Ray Jerome Baker shortly after their marriage in March, 1873

Baker's first photo, taken in Austin, Minnesota, June, 1888

es to give any thought to a desire to follow his occupation, but my interest in what went on and the pictures which followed no doubt constituted one of the building blocks of interest which later on caused me to choose photography as life's profession."

Another incident that Baker recalled was the visit to the Austin farm of a young man who was working his way through college as a traveling photographer. At the rear of his horse and buggy he had built a small darkroom so that he could stand on the ground and work in the dark with his chemicals. He used a large plate camera to shoot several pictures of the farm before driving back into town. A week later he returned to the farm with the finished sepia prints mounted on white cardboard. They cost a dollar each.

In 1898, Baker went away to St. Paul and for the next four years attended Mechanic Arts High School. There he shot his first photographs with a 4x5 plate camera that was owned by the husband of one of his sisters. He developed his pictures in the bathroom of a schoolmate who shared his enthusiasm for photography.

After completing a semester at the University of Minnesota in 1903, Baker became a traveling photographer, himself. He spent that winter in Portland, Oregon and then worked his way down the coast, arriving in Eureka, California, in October, 1904.

Eureka was a logging town in those days with a half-dozen sawmills. Baker rented a vacant lot on E Street and erected a tent on the property. This temporary photographic studio worked fine in dry weather but was a mess in the rain.

The situation got better when Ed Chase, a fellow photographer who had a studio a few blocks away, sold Baker his portrait camera, background cloths and other equipment. Baker continued in Chase's former location on the corner of E and 5th Streets until he moved to Hawaii.

During his residence in Eureka, Baker bought himself a motorcycle and a sidecar to hold his camera. He then hired a girl to look after the studio while he went out to the logging camps and took pictures of the lumberjacks. These workers wanted photographs to send back to

Edith Baker, Earl Frost Baker and Ray Jerome Baker, 1919

Ray Jerome Baker acquired this camera in 1906 and it was used all of his career in Hawaii, 1908

their families. Baker also took a considerable number of Indian portraits and a series of photographs of the giant redwood trees.

Baker, as portraits of the time indicate, was a handsome young man who stood 5 feet, 6 inches tall. His brown hair was parted in the middle over a high forehead and he wore round, wire-rim glasses in front of hazel eyes.

We know little about his courtship with Edith Mary Frost, a local schoolteacher, but they were married on November 21, 1906. They had apparently met at a Socialist Party meeting in Eureka.

Jack London, a writer who had catapulted to fame with the recently published novels *The Call of the Wild* (1903), *The Sea-Wolf* (1904) and *White Fang* (1906) was also a Socialist Party member. After his 1907 trip to Hawaii he spoke favorably to the Bakers of the islands he had visited.

Baker and his wife decided to see for themselves and in February, 1908 they came to Honolulu on a delayed wedding trip. Their ship was the steamer *Mongolia*, later known as the *President Fillmore*. Among the other passen-

gers was Ella Wheeler Wilcox, a poet known for her passionate verse.

One day, as the steamer neared Honolulu, Mrs. Wilcox entered the social hall "adorned in the inevitable chiffon veils" and set up a card table. Baker wrote later that "she stacked her letters high and kept one of the Chinese stewards busy bringing stamps and running errands."

Mrs. Wilcox, like the Bakers, checked into the Alexander Young Hotel where she was "showered with attention." Before she departed again on the steamer a reception was held "attended by the elite" where some of her poems were "admiringly read."

Baker and his wife extended their planned two-week visit to four months. One of Edith's cousins was married to the son of William Faucett Pogue, a Maui plantation irrigation specialist. Pogue opened the doors of Maui society for Baker and recommended the photographer's work to his friends. One of the assignments he got was to take pictures of the von Tempsky family at their ranch on Haleakala.

Years later Baker enjoyed pulling out a photo

Ray Jerome Baker took this self-portrait on his wedding day, Nov. 21, 1906

Baker's studio on Kalakaua Avenue, 1920

showing the young daughter, Armine, with an arm around her favorite colt. Armine von Tempski (she preferred an "i" in her last name) grew up to become the author of the autobiographical *Born in Paradise* and such well-known Hawaii novels as *Dust, Hula, Fire* and *Lava*. She died in 1943, of somewhat mysterious circumstances, in a Fresno, California, hotel room.

After their trip to the Neighbor Islands, the Bakers returned to Oahu and a quieter routine. Baker remembered that "in Honolulu we took quarters in a private home at 236 South King Street. Across the street stood a giant monkey-pod tree which marked the site of the present Hawaiian Electric office building. A rear portion of the lot overlooked the lovely grounds of a prominent Hawaiian family and has long since become the site of Honolulu's Y.W.C.A."

The room rented by the Bakers was actually located at the corner of King and Richards St. The house had been built and formerly occupied by Bruce Cartwright, the son of Alexander Cartwright who had been Honolulu's first fire-chief and the founder of the game of baseball.

After their four-month stay, the Bakers sailed back to California. By now they had made up their minds to move permanently to Hawaii and once back in Eureka they began making preparations for the switch. In 1909, their only child, Earl Frost Baker, was born.

The Bakers returned to Honolulu in February of 1910. They rented a house in Kaimuki for seven months (one of their neighbors was young Buster Crabbe) and, after yet another mainland visit, rented a cottage at 1679 Beach Road—near the present Kaiser Hospital and Marina Theatres—for $25 a month.

In the early years of his Hawaii residence, Baker's primary interest was in photographing the Hawaiians and their environment. "The Hawaiian people were so unspoiled," he wrote in his autobiography, "so unsophisticated, and the children so unconscious of attention that the gathering of photographic records of early Hawaiian life was easy and a pleasure. It just so happened that no one had done it before."

"Hawaiian men threw their nets, handled their spears, pounded poi or worked their taro patches and launched their canoes with realism,

Earl Frost Baker, playing in the yard of his father's home on Beach Road, 1911. Now Ala Moana Boulevard, site of the Kaiser Hospital.

Baker's studio at 1911 Kalakaua in 1937. This glass cage which was added in 1935 to display his pictures and books was a popular landmark for passersby. Today, in 1982, the Kalakauan Hotel is located on the site.

completely unconscious of the attention shown them. Nor did they demand exorbitant fees for having a few pictures made of them. In fact, I considered that when Hawaiian subjects began to demand payment for having pictures made, they lost their value as subjects."

Baker had met James J. Williams, a Honolulu photographer, during his 1908 trip and they remained close friends from then on. They often took trips around the island together to photograph various sites and events. Once, when Baker was short on supplies, Williams sold him about 1500 used glass plates. Baker scraped the emulsion off about 300 of the plates and reused those that he felt did not have historical value. The others he put safely aside.

Williams was a busy man and had a staff of several photographers to help him cover important social events. Baker often worked for Williams on specific assignments, one of the first being the 1913 celebration of Kamehameha the Great's landing on Oahu.

"Canoes were apparently more abundant then than later," Baker wrote years afterwards,

"and a considerable fleet of them was assembled for the great warrior's invading army. There was, however, another difficulty which at the moment seemed unsurmountable: the carry-over of missionary prudishness had affected the Hawaiian men in such a way that they were very reluctant to show their bare skin, as had been customary in Kamehameha's time. The only alternative was to fit them out with knit underwear, dyed brown."

Baker also took motion pictures. In 1910 he had been given film lessons by Thomas Edison during a visit to the inventor's East Coast laboratories and Edison encouraged him to take motion pictures in Hawaii. His first film was of a hula dancer that unfortunately no longer exists.

In early 1913, Baker and a fellow photographer, E. L. Edgeworth, formed a co-partnership to operate a studio at the corner of Kalakaua Avenue and Ena Road. In November, 1913, the partnership was dissolved and Baker continued the photographic business by himself.

Baker and his wife remained on Beach Road until 1915. The trouble began after they bought a new Packard. When the landlady saw the car

The first of the famed "Rusty the Cat" cats who were commentators of the social mores of our times. Baker's studio, 1926

The Interior of Baker's studio-residence. The backdrop and camera were used all of Baker's photographic career, 1940

she decided that they were making too much money in the photographic business. She raised the rent and it wasn't long before the Bakers gave notice and moved out.

They then rented and eventually purchased property at 1911 Kalakaua Avenue, near the corner of John Ena Road. It consisted of about 5000 square-feet of land with a house that they used for both a residence and photo studio. In later years they were also able to purchase the adjoining lots at 1915 and 1923 Kalakaua Ave.

In 1914 Baker also began making lantern slides. He re-photographed his black and white still pictures and afterwards his wife hand-colored the new positives for screen projection. On May 12 and 13, 1914 he had his first major slide showings in downtown Honolulu at the Opera House. He hired a vocal group to sing Hawaiian songs as slides flashed on the screen. After the hall rental and other expenses were paid his profit amounted to only $1.50. He blamed the low attendance on poor publicity.

Two years later, Baker took a steamer to Japan, arriving in Yokohama after a ten-day voyage. While in Japan he climbed Mt. Fuji-yama and then continued on to Korea in July.

During this trip he made over 600 negatives, only about 50 of which have ever been published.

In 1918 there was a major volcanic eruption on the Big Island and Baker went over to shoot the crater, the inside of which had become a lake of molten lava. This was the first time motion pictures had been taken of a Kilauea eruption and, to make it even more spectacular, he hand-colored each frame of the developed negative. He thus produced the world's first-known "color" motion pictures.

From 1915 to 1919, Baker also produced ten short films about Hawaii for the Ford Educational Series, a weekly film program distributed through the school system. He received about $1 a foot for these short ten-minute films which he shot and supplied caption material for the editors in Hollywood.

During the late summer of 1919, Baker worked for the Midland Chautauqua Circuit, headquartered in Des Moines, Iowa. This company booked entertainment and lectures for the states of Iowa, Minnesota, Wisconsin, the Dakotas, Nebraska and Kansas.

Baker traveled with a group called the Ameri-

The Interior of Baker's studio-residence, 1940

Ray Jerome Baker on the *Palmyra*, leaving for Palmyra Island on June 3, 1922

can Ladies Quartet. They wore bright costumes and sang patriotic songs for the small-town audiences. Usually they performed in the late afternoon, accompanied by a piano, and set the stage for Baker's evening showing of lantern slides and motion pictures.

Lecturing on *Hawaii, Land of Heart's Desire*, Baker was able to make $750 to $1,000 a month through his shows. The Oceanic Steamship Co. provided free passage between the mainland and Hawaii each summer, but all of his other expenses had to be covered by an admission charge of 50 cents.

Baker stayed on the circuit for only two seasons. "After 1920," he recalled, "I did not attempt to renew my contract with the company, for it seemed to me that with the improvement of motion pictures, theatres, and highways, there was little promise for the future."

Until 1935, Baker took movies of countless events that took place in Hawaii. For a number of years he maintained his own laboratory where he developed film and made prints for sale to libraries and collectors.

Baker's motion pictures, like his still photography, provide a fascinating look at early 20th

century Hawaii. He covered the arrival of "Daisy," the Honolulu Zoo elephant in 1916, Queen Liliuokalani's last birthday and funeral in 1917, Prince Jonah Kuhio Kalanianaole's funeral in 1922 and former governor Sanford B. Dole turning 80 in 1924.

In 1925 he visited Australia and New Zealand, filming for Pathe News along the way. When a Navy cruiser, the USS Chicago, made a shakedown cruise through the South Pacific in 1931, he was invited to come aboard and make a documentary record of the voyage which included stops at Tahiti and Samoa.

Baker did little motion picture work after shooting the arrival of the first China Clipper passenger plane in 1935. Sound movies had arrived and his hobby was becoming too costly.

Tragedy entered Baker's life on October 9, 1938 when Edith suffered a paralytic stroke. He had gone outside to the car that morning and returned to find her lying unconscious on the floor of the pantry. She was in the hospital a month, then a private nursing home for about a year. In 1940, a sister from California took her to the mainland, but she never fully recovered from the stroke.

Ray Jerome Baker upon his graduation from the University of Hawaii, 1934

Ray Jerome Baker, "going native" in Japan, 1917

Baker filming with his motion picture camera, 1926

On Dec. 7, 1941 the Japanese attacked Pearl Harbor and the next day it became illegal to take any photos showing outdoor scenes that might be of value to the enemy. Throughout the war years, however, Baker kept busy taking portraits of servicemen stationed here or heading overseas. Other income was derived from over a dozen rental units. Seldom were any of the units vacant for more than a day.

Baker found out, however, that the life of a landlord had its drawbacks. One day after giving a tenant an eviction notice—she owed several months of rent payments—the woman and her sister entered his office and physically attacked him.

According to a report Baker filed with the police, they "began pummeling me, tore my ear, dented a face powder can which was handy and one of them landed a heavy blow which cut my shirt and caused swelling. I was no match for the infuriated women and ran from them."

After the war, the quality of Baker's tenants improved but he photographed less. He preferred to produce limited edition books of his past work and to take new pictures abroad. In 1949 he toured Mexico, in 1951 the West Indies and in 1952, Alaska. He took trips to Central America in 1953, South America in 1955, Europe in 1956, New Zealand in 1957 and the Soviet Union in 1958.

During the 1950's, Baker began thinking of the future and started giving much of his photographs, motion pictures and equipment to Robert E. Van Dyke. Van Dyke was then only in his early teens but he was already a major collector of Hawaiiana.

Van Dyke encouraged Baker to make a photographic trip to the Neighbor Islands in 1960 and accompanied him to Kauai, Maui and the Big Island. The photographs taken during this trip represent his last significant series of work.

In 1960 Baker also made out his will, assigning his remaining photographs, books and equipment to the Bernice P. Bishop Museum. His properties on Kalakaua Avenue were left to the museum as well and he intended their rental income would establish and maintain a "Ray Jerome Baker Room" devoted to photography in the Islands.

The backyard of the Baker studio on Dudoit Lane. The two-story garage building was the motion picture studio.

Baker in his motion picture drying room, 1932

Baker in his studio doing scientific studies with his assistant Morgan Reynolds. Baker mans the microscope, Reynolds the motion picture camera, 1932

Baker died at age 91 on Oct. 27, 1972. He had outlived both his wife and son. Upon his death the Bishop Museum accepted his estate and preparations were made to honor his request. On July 17, 1979, the public was invited to the grand opening of the Ray Jerome Baker Room which contains his work and that of others who have photographed in Hawaii.

The will also asked that a plaque be exhibited at the museum with the following words. "In order that the people may forever remember the beauty of old Hawaii and as an inspiration to the people to help perpetuate the present beauty of Hawaii, I have endowed this room and provided for the development of the pictorial history of Hawaii here shown."

It is still too soon, of course, to measure Baker's full contribution to photography in Hawaii. Like many great artists he was ahead of his time. The importance of his work, as the photographs in this book clearly show, will only increase as the years go by.

To Robert

I feel that I have been a most fortunate person, for I have had a hobby for my occupation for more than fifty years. It has given me a modest living; I never expected it to make me rich, but it has made me happy. My life has been rich and full and satisfying. I have memories to last me as long as I live

Ray Jerome Baker

Dec 11, 1957

Inscription in a book to Robert E. Van Dyke

Baker found beauty in routine jobs—such as farming, fishing, and cooking—and the manner of their execution.

Woman weaving lauhala hat near Onomea, Hawaii, 1916

HAWAIIAN WAYS

Almost from the moment he first saw the Islands in 1908, Ray Jerome Baker was fascinated by the Hawaiians, the first people who had come onto these shores. He tried to learn everything he could about their history, customs and lifestyle.

Only 15 years earlier, in 1893, the monarchy had been overthrown. Hawaiians could still remember the day that their flag had come down at Iolani Palace and the events surrounding Queen Liliuokalani's dethronement had made them angry and confused. Without their accustomed rulers, they found it increasingly difficult to preserve their heritage and sense of cultural identity.

When Captain James Cook visited Hawaii in 1778, his officers estimated the population by taking the average number of persons in each house and multiplying that figure by the average number of houses in each village. Estimates ranged from a low of 242,000 to a high of 400,000.

The number was likely somewhere inbetween. In 1823, the missionary William Ellis reported a Hawaiian population of about 140,000. By the 1872 census the number had dropped to 57,000 with only 44,000 of these being full-blooded Hawaiians.

The Hawaiians and their ways were vanishing and Baker realized the loss. He regularly visited local families, using his cameras to record what remained. In the more remote areas he found that farming and fishing were still important parts of the Hawaiian lifestyle. Grass houses, though they were becoming scarce, were built for shelter and wooden canoes were a common means of transportation.

For Baker the early 20th century Hawaiian was generally a romantic figure. His photographic studies, thoughtfully arranged, were extensions of this idealistic approach. If he saw fishermen near the water or a group of hula dancers, he did not hesitate to ask them to straighten their nets or pose in a certain way.

Baker was fascinated by how people worked, played and went about their daily lives. He found beauty in routine jobs—such as farming, fishing and cooking—and the manner of their execution. His photographs go a step beyond merely showing how the Hawaiians wove lauhala mats or prepared a pig for the luau. They capture, too, the inner pride and satisfaction.

The pictures of Ray Jerome Baker are seldom confused with those of his contemporaries who worked in Hawaii. His approach was uniquely his own and his photographs remain unmatched in communicating the individual self-respect and spirit of the Hawaiian people.

Woman in front of grass shack near Halawa, Molokai, 1912

Grass shack near Kilauea, Kauai, 1914

Grass shack near Kilauea, Kauai, 1914

Grass shack near Hanalei, Kauai, 1912

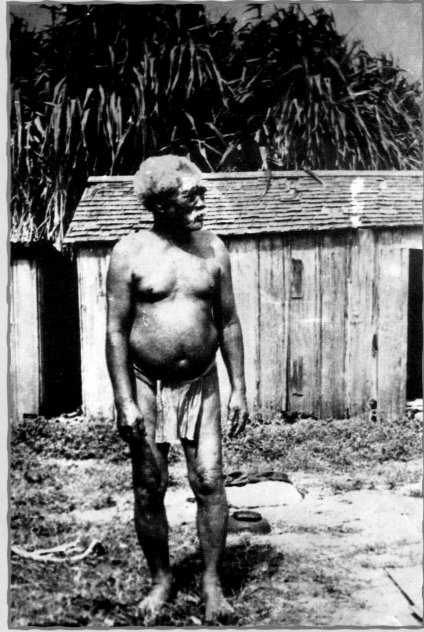

Old Hawaiian wearing a malo, Kona, Hawaii, 1910

Hawaiian girls group with ukuleles and guitars, 1908

Two Hawaiian men preparing the pig and laulaus for a luau, 1912

Hawaiian women weaving a lauhala mat, 1912

Hawaiian woman washing hala leaves, Molokai, 1914

Two Hawaiian men pounding poi, Kauai, 1918

Hawaiian throw-net fisherman, Kauai, 1914

During the early years of this century the Hawaiian fisherman with his spear or throw-net was still a common sight in the Islands. Many of them belonged to families which had long specialized in collecting the rich, varied and abundant harvests of the oceans around these islands.

These families knew the secrets of the sea and how to catch fish. They were proud of their experience and technique and passed their knowledge on from generation to generation.

Ray Jerome Baker appreciated the importance of fishing to the Hawaiian culture. He enjoyed meeting these men during his walks along the shoreline and, over his long career, took many pictures of them.

Hawaiian girls sitting on a mat, 1912

Hawaiian girls eating poi while one plays on a nose flute, 1912

Hawaiian girls on a mat weaving lauhala, 1912

Hawaiian girls pounding tapa cloth, 1912

Hawaiian girl dressed in hula costume, Kohala, Hawaii, 1912

Hula dancer in outdoor setting, 1912

Hawaiian fishermen near Lahaina, Maui, 1908

Hawaiian fisherwoman on the beach, Maui, 1915

Hawaiian woman with lauhala for mat
weaving, Pukoo, Molokai, 1912

Hula dancer in studio setting, 1912

17 —

Hukilau catch, being placed in a basket, Oahu, 1915

Hula girl, Baker Studio, 1930

Pau rider at the Ward Estate, 1910

Woman fishing for Opai (shrimp),
Kauai, 1914

Hawaiian woman with net for *Opai*, Kauai, 1914

Hawaiian woman washing clothes in stream near Paia, Maui, 1912

Hawaiian Lady, Pukoo, Molokai, 1912

Adele Robinson (Mrs. Herman Lemke), as a Pau rider, Old Plantation, 1910

Hawaiian boy weaving a coconut hat on the grounds of the Royal Hawaiian Hotel, 1929

Hawaiian boy climbing a coconut tree near Lahaina, 1912

Two men in outrigger canoe, Lahaina, Maui, 1914

Hawaiian man with net near Halawa Valley, Molokai, 1912

Hawaiian man with a fish net near Halawa Valley, Molokai, 1912

Man leaning on Pandanus tree, Molokai, 1912

Hawaiian girl photographed at the request of Dr. Emerson to use as a photographic interpretation of Hiiaka, sister of Pele, Waimea, Kauai, 1912.

Baker treated all people as equals while recognizing at the same time that each minority group in Hawaii had its own traditional customs and outlook.

PEOPLE

During the 1930's, one of Baker's most popular mainland lectures was entitled "*People of Hawaii*." During his talk he gave a brief history of Hawaii, describing how the various ethnic groups arrived. He illustrated the lecture with 250 hand-colored lantern slides and original motion picture film.

"For twenty-five years I have made my home in Hawaii," Baker wrote in 1934. "It is a place where the culture of the East meets that of the West, where races meet and mingle, both in a social and in a biological sense. It is a place where a primitive Polynesian background furnishes the matrix on which the eastern and western cultures are mixed and blended. It is there that one of the most daring and interesting experiments in human biology in the world today is going on."

Baker was, quite simply, a man without real prejudice. He treated all people as equals while recognizing at the same time that each minority group in Hawaii had its own traditional customs and outlook. He didn't always understand them —sometimes he was even a bit annoyed—but he took all of his ethnic experiences with grace and good humor.

In 1939 he took a course in "Race Relations" from Dr. Andrew Lind at the University of Hawaii. He enjoyed it immensely. For one class project Lind asked him to interview people about racial attitudes and he came away from the study with the realization that, despite surface differences, all of Hawaii's people were basically the same.

Besides his pictures of the "common man," Baker took photographs of prominent residents like Queen Liliuokalani, Sanford B. Dole, Alexander Hume Ford and Duke Kahanamoku. Among the famous visitors he photographed were George Bernard Shaw, Christopher Morley, and Carl Sandburg.

In later years his clearest memories were probably of the writer Jack London who had visited Hawaii in 1907, a year before Baker arrived. He stopped at Honolulu again in 1915 and 1916 with his wife, Charmian, and they rented a cottage on Beach Walk in Waikiki. London was then at the height of his fame, the highest paid and most popular author in the world.

Baker was a frequent guest in London's cottage and he took a number of photographs of the famous author during his stay. After a big farewell party the Londons sailed from Hawaii on July 26, 1916. He was never to return. Four months later, at his ranch in Glen Ellen, California, Jack London died of uremic poisoning. Into his grave was thrown a withered ilima lei that had been given to him in Hawaii.

Hawaiian girl, Lahaina, 1912

Hawaiian girl, 1922

Hawaiian girl, Honolulu, 1908

Hawaiian girl, Maui 1912

Hawaiian girl, Hawaii 1912

Hawaiian fisherwomen on the beach, Maui, 1915

Hawaiian woman on the beach, Honolulu, 1914

Hawaiian girl, Baker's studio, 1930

Hawaiian girl, Hawaii, 1913

Hawaiian girl wearing lokelani lei, Honolulu, 1912

Hawaiian woman on the beach, Maui, 1914

Hawaiian woman on beach near
Kaunakakai, Molokai, 1912

Chinese Hawaiian farmer, Hawaii, 1916

Hawaiian girl, Baker Studio, 1930

On the trail, Hawaii, 1920

Children on the beach, Waimea, Kauai, 1915

Hawaiian girl on the beach, Waimea, Kauai, 1915

Hawaiian woman, Molokai, 1912

Hawaiian woman, Hawaii, 1916

Hunter carrying a wild boar, Waipio, Hawaii, 1916

Hawaiian woman,
Molokai, 1912

Hawaiian-Chinese man, Hawaii, 1918

Hawaiian man selling fruit, Hawaii, 1912

Shy Hawaiian girl on a Kona nightingale, Kona, 1908

Children on the beach, Waimea, Kauai, 1915

Hawaiian children on the beach, Waimea, Kauai, 1914

Hawaiian girl in wet clothes on Kauai, 1915

Shy Hawaiian girl on the beach, Kauai, 1914

Hawaiian girls, Waimea, Kauai, 1912

Boy wearing a hat, Hawaii, 1912

Hawaiian child, Maui, 1914

Hawaiian boys from the neighborhood
in Baker's studio, 1930

Hawaiian boy on beach, Kauai, 1914

Hawaiian child, Maui, 1914

Hula Dancers, 1927

Two Hula Dancers with studio
backdrops, 1927

Young Hula Dancer in a studio setting, 1927

Hula Dancer in outdoor setting, 1927

Hula Dancer, 1927   Hula Dancer in studio, 1927   Hawaiian girl, 1927

A young Hula troupe, 1927

When hula was in its heyday of revival, Rose Heather exemplified everything that Hula wasn't. She was a Canadian beauty, totally without Hawaiian blood and she had never seen Hawaii before 1918. She and Baker created this series of pictures in 1921 for advertising purposes.

Although Baker found his greatest satisfaction in taking pictures of the common person, he seldom missed an opportunity to photograph the well-known. Whenever he heard that visiting celebrities were in town, he would seek them out with his camera.

A few of the people in these pictures have quite familiar faces. The rest were famous only in Hawaii. They were all chosen for this section because they held a special meaning to Baker.

Some of them, like Duke Kahanamoku and Jack London, were close friends. Others, like the Prince of Wales and Carl Sandburg, crossed his life but once—and yet their memory, caught in these photographs, remains forever.

Famous People

Norman Ross, former world's long distance freestyle swimming champion, and Duke Kahanamoku, in front of the Hustace residence in Waikiki, 1920.

Duke Kahanamoku and Amelia Earhart eating a pineapple, 1935

Duke Kahanamoku as Sheriff of Honolulu, 1935

Duke Kahanamoku photographed at Baker's studio, 1932

Mark Twain (born Samuel Clemens) came to Hawaii in 1866 as a 31-year-old journalist on assignment for the *Sacramento Union*. He spent four months and a day exploring the Sandwich Islands, as they were called then, and sent back a humorous series of 25 travel letters that appeared in the daily and weekend editions of the newspaper.

The young reporter later used these letters as the basis for a major section of his first book, *Roughing it*, which was published six years after he returned to the mainland. Twain never got a chance to revisit Hawaii but in time he would write such classics as *Tom Sawyer* and *Huckleberry Finn* and become one of the most famous authors in the world.

In 1909, Baker took this photograph at Twain's High Victorian Gothic mansion in Hartford Connecticut. He posed Twain with a pipe in his hand wearing the familiar white suit that had become his trademark.

Although this photograph was not taken in Hawaii it was one of Baker's favorites and is of historical importance. Less than a year after it was taken, Mark Twain died at the age of seventy five.

Mark Twain at his home in Connecticutt, 1909

H.R.H. the Prince of Wales, right, and his cousin, Louis Mountbatten, visiting Iolani Palace, 1920

Buster Crabbe, swimming champion and star of "Tarzan" and "Flash Gordon" films, leaves for college with his brother, 1927

Eben Low, famous cowboy and rancher, 1938

Henri Berger, organizer and conductor of the Royal Hawaiian Band, and his daughter, Lehua, 1912

Carl Sandburg, poet and Lincoln scholar, and his wife, Paula, plant a tree at the University of Hawaii, 1934

Julia Judd Swanzy, civic leader and philanthropist, 1918

Mrs. Willis Marks, actress, at the Waimea River on Kauai, 1912

William Tufts Brigham, founding director of the Bernice P. Bishop Museum, at his residence at the corner of School and Emma streets, 1922

Jennie Kapahu Wilson, premier hula dancer at the court of King Kalakaua and wife of Honolulu Mayor John H. Wilson, 1934

James Drummond Dole, founder of Dole Pineapple, and family, 1924

Opera singer Madame Ululani, later Mrs. A.G.M. Robertson and then Mrs. Jan Jabulka, 1918

Judge and Mrs. Walter Frear at their Punahou Street residence, Arcadia, 1946

Christopher Morley—poet, novelist and playwright—plants a tree at McKinley High School, 1933

Louis von Tempsky and his son, 1908

—38

Samuel Wilder King, delegate to congress, and his wife, Pauline Evans King, campaigning in Papakolea, 1934

John Poole, purchaser and subdivider of Princess Kaiulani's home at "Ainahau," 1922

Alice Poole, wife of John Poole and one of the first staff members of the Honolulu Academy of Arts, 1922

Bud Mars, after making the first airplane flight in Hawaii at the Polo Field on the Damon Estate at Moanalua, Dec. 31, 1910

Alexander Hume Ford, founder of "Mid Pacific Magazine" (1911-1936), the Outrigger Canoe Club and the Hawaiian Trail and Mountain Club, at his desk in the Stangenwald Building, 1914

Armine von Tempski and her favorite colt, 1908

von Tempsky family, 1910

Alice Roosevelt Longworth, daughter of President Theodore Roosevelt, at the Pali Lookout, 1911

Mrs. Willis Marks strikes a dance pose at the Damon Estate at Moanalua, 1912

Mrs. Willis Marks at the Damon Estate at Moanalua, 1912

Jack London at the Scott cottage on Beachwalk Avenue, Waikiki, 1915

Charmian and Jack London and her cousin Bess Kittredge at the Scott residence, 1915

Jack and Charmian London at the Outrigger Canoe Club, 1915

Jack London wrote two volumes of short stories set in Hawaii, *The House of Pride* and *On the Makaloa Mat*. They contain some of his finest writing about the Pacific.

London saw Hawaii for the first time in 1893 while a deckhand on a passing sealing ship. In 1904, traveling as a correspondent in the Russo-Japanese War, he stopped here on his way to the Orient and, again, six months later on his way back to California.

Returning to Hawaii in 1907 aboard his private yacht, the *Snark*, London and his wife, Charmian, divided their four-month stay between a bungalow near Pearl City and a cottage on the grounds of the old Seaside Hotel in Waikiki. He learned how to surf from Alexander Hume Ford, George Freeth and other new-found friends.

During a trip to Maui, the Londons rode horseback with Louis von Tempsky, who had a cattle ranch on the slopes of Haleakala. One of von Tempsky's daughters, 14-year-old Armine, was especially impressed by London and grew up to be a well-known author herself.

In 1915, at the height of his fame as a writer, London and his wife returned and spent almost a year in Hawaii. By then Baker was living in Honolulu and he took a number of photographs of the couple. Some have been widely published, others have not.

London returned to Honolulu for a brief time in early 1916 and he asked Baker to supply some photographs to illustrate some magazine article he was writing about Hawaii. One day they had lunch together at The Hau Tree Inn, later the Halekulani Hotel, and talked about the project.

The writer picked out some of Baker's photographs and returned with them to California in late summer, 1916. London's articles were still unfinished when London died that November at the age of forty.

Jack London at the Scott Cottage on Beachwalk Avenue, Waikiki, 1915

Kamehameha Day Parade, King Street, 1932

Kamehameha Day Parade, King Street, 1932

Army Air Force in Review, 1926

Japanese and American officials reviewing troops,
Wheeler Field, 1929

Lifestyle

One of the things Baker liked best about Hawaii was its diversity of ethnic groups. While the Japanese, Chinese, Portuguese and Filipinos seemed to blend together in harmony, each group retained its unique cultural identity.

Baker spent considerable time walking around Chinatown and the other urban ethnic communities with his camera. The street merchants, in particular, interested him. He also visited the rural plantations on a regular basis to take pictures of the people living there.

The photographs on these pages are representative of the hundreds that might be grouped under the category of "Lifestyle." Some obviously look dated. Others, with a simple change of clothes, might have been taken yesterday. Several probably could be identified with similar scenes of the time photographed anywhere in the U.S.

Men from Palama area, 1932

Chinese jewelry store on Hotel and Maunakea streets, 1932

Chinese neighborhood market in Chinatown, 1932

Maunakea Street hardware and grocery store, 1932

The shoe shine boys on Hotel at Maunakea, 1932

Shoe shine boys on Hotel and Maunakea streets, 1932

Vegetable delivery wagon on John Ena Road, 1932

Chinese vegetable peddler on Maunakea Street, 1932

Paper boys selling the "Pacific Commercial Advertiser" on Alakea Street, near Hotel Street, 1916

Portuguese man and a Filipino man in Palama, 1932

Hardware and grocery store on Maunakea Street, 1932

Neighborhood fish delivery wagon, Honolulu, 1932

Traffic cop at King and Fort Street, 1916

Chinese neighborhood market, Chinatown, 1932

Plantation workers watch a sumo-wrestling contest, Lahaina, Maui, 1908

Japanese carp streamers fly on Boy's Day, Lahaina, Maui, 1922

Firemen doing the hula at Central Fire Station, 1935

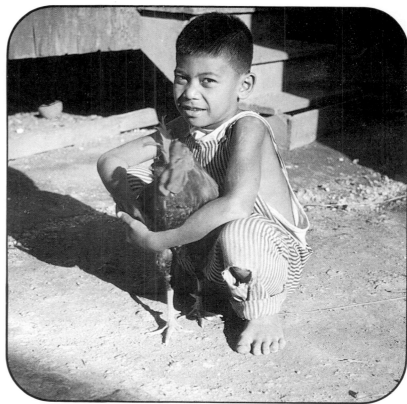

Boy with his prize fighting cock, Ewa Plantation, 1932

Filipino women in the plantation village, Oahu Sugar Co., 1932

Children in their Sunday best, 1926

Children playing in homemade swimming pool, 1934

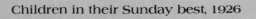

Plantation children on the way home from school, Waialua, Oahu, 1930

Plantation children on their school playground, 1932

Chinese children in Chinatown, 1932

Plantation children, 1924

Plantation children, 1915

Mother & beautiful daughters, 1930

Portugese-Hawaiian children, 1912

Boy in yard, 1930

College girls, 1930

Filipino woman in ceremonial dress, Waipahu, 1932

Japanese girl and her doll, 1924

Chinese family, 1930

Japanese bride and her attendants, 1926

Chinese girl, 1930

Queen Liliuokalani, at the dedication of Pearl Harbor, Dec. 15, 1911

Governor Lucius Pinkam at Iolani Palace, 1914

Queen Liliuokalani lying in state at Kawaiahao Church, Nov. 1917

Royalty
Queen Liliuokalani

The last ruler of the Hawaiian kingdom, and the only woman to rule it alone, was Queen Liliuokalani. She succeeded her older brother, David Kalakaua, to the throne in 1891.

Queen Liliuokalani was unsuccessful in her attempt to restore the power of the monarchy that had been lost when King Kalakaua was forced to sign the Constitution of 1887. In trying to proclaim a new Constitution she angered the American residents of the Islands who forced her abdication in 1893.

On July 4, 1894, the Republic of Hawaii was declared. Less than a year afterwards the Queen was arrested for treason in a plot to overthrow the Republic of Hawaii. She then renounced all claims to the throne to win clemency for those who had participated in the plot.

The dethroned Queen lived the rest of her life quietly at Washington Place. Baker took a number of photographs of Liliuokalani until her death in 1917, and possibly the only motion picture of her at her 79th birthday on September 2, 1917.

Queen Liliuokalani, 1916

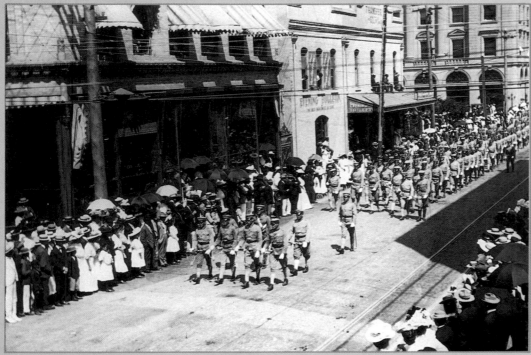

Funeral procession of Prince David Kawananakoa. Passing
on King Street, June 1908

Prince Jonah Kuhio Kalanianaole lying in state in the Throne Room of Iolani Palace, 1922

At the time of his visit to Hawaii in 1908, Ray Jerome Baker was on hand to photograph the funeral of Prince David Kawananakoa, a nephew of the former Queen Kapiolani, and considered by many to be the titular heir apparent to the now gone Hawaiian throne.

Baker would nine years later make the only existing motion pictures of Hawaii's last monarch, Queen Liliuokalani, on the occasion of her final birthday, September 2, 1917. Several months later, in November, 1917, he would film the Queen's funeral procession.

In 1922, Baker took several hundred still photos of the funeral of Prince Jonah Kuhio Kalanianaole, last heir to the throne of Hawaii. Baker had thus witnessed the passing of the last three members of the Hawaiian royal family and before him passed the ceremonial splendor of the closing of the Hawaiian monarchy.

Funeral procession of Prince Jonah Kuhio Kalanianaole. The catafalque leaving Iolani Palace and proceeding up King Street, 1922

On the morning of Dec. 7, 1941, Ray Jerome Baker was at the house of a neighbor, preparing for a drive into the country. When he first heard the bombs and gunfire he thought it was target practice. Later a radio announcer came on the air to announce that Pearl Harbor had been attacked by Japanese planes.

In the days immediately following, martial law was declared. Baker reported to a school in Waikiki where he was registered and finger-printed. Honolulu was put under curfew and at night the city was completely blacked out. Certain foods and gasoline were rationed.

As the excitement died down and the war

dragged on, personal cameras were taken off the market completely. What pictures were taken were likely to be censored. As a result of the drastic increase in Honolulu's transient population, Baker and his fellow photographers found themselves working day and night taking portraits of servicemen. Under ordinary circumstances, few of these men would have had their pictures taken. But as they headed into the Pacific they faced an uncertain future. Encouraged by their parents, wives and sweethearts, they kept the studios busy with appointments.

Sadly, however, many of these young men

Faces of the 1940's

did not come back. Baker sometimes would receive letters from their family and relatives requesting copies of the photos he'd taken while they were in Honolulu. He promptly looked through his files and sent them any additional proofs or negatives.

During the war years Baker employed a pretty, young Filipino girl to help out in his studio. She was an orphan, raised by a Caucasian family, and married to a part-Hawaiian pineapple factory worker. Baker developed a fondness for the girl, paid her $25 a week, and taught her how to take portraits by herself when he had other work to do. Her real name was Connie but Baker and

the boys in uniform nicknamed her "Sunshine" because of her outgoing personality.

Waikiki, of course, was forever changed by the war. Many of the men who had seen the Islands during their tours of duty took their military discharges here and the population of Hawaii rose dramatically. Waikiki Beach was no longer a place where friends stopped and chatted. It was now a place full of strangers and Baker felt uncomfortably out of place. After the war ended, his studio business fell off considerably and he took few portraits. Most of his photographic work during the late 1940's and 1950's was directed toward his book projects.

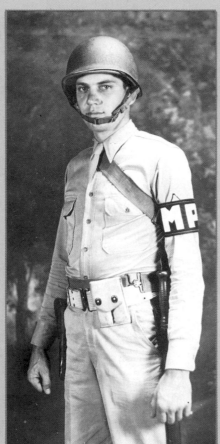

Today they are mostly nameless faces in the archives of Mr. Baker but, from 1942 thru 1945, they were the backbone of America. They came to Hawaii by the thousands and by the thousands they trooped through the door of 1915 Kalakaua Ave. More often than not the visit to Baker's studio was not done on their own but, at the request of parents, wives and girl friends. To many it would be their last photo, a living treasure to the past.

Two soldiers pose in front of a Library of Hawaii bomb shelter, 1943

Kodak Hawaii notice on the illegality of taking photographs, signed by the Military Governor of Hawaii

Remains of the abandoned army camp at the base of Nuuanu Pali. 1945

A crowd of sailors outside the Hawaii Theater, 1943

The Black Cat, a popular bar across from the Armed Forces YMCA, 1943

Nothing else in the city's history has ever matched the frenzied excitement and celebration of Boat Days.

Streamers, a last farewell, the sounds of the Royal Hawaiian Band, Aloha Oe and we are off, 1928

BOAT DAYS

For many years the arrivals and departures of Honolulu's passenger ships were gala social events. Musicians played, hula girls swayed and visitors cried beneath a deluge of leis and paper confetti. Flags and streamers flew everywhere. Nothing else in the city's history has ever matched the frenzied excitement and celebration of Boat Days.

It is hard to imagine now in this age of jet airplane service, but during the first half of this century Honolulu's regular routine almost stopped when the big Matson ships came in. As soon as Hawaiian Electric Company's whistle sounded, people dropped whatever they were doing and hurried over to the harbor in order to welcome the newcomers.

Canoe paddlers escorted the vessel to shore and beach boys swam out to dive for coins tossed overboard. Waiting majestically on the wharf, playing familiar island tunes, was the Royal Hawaiian Band.

Baker knew people on both the *Pacific Commercial Advertiser* and the *Star-Bulletin* in those days. Whenever a boat left San Francisco, Castle & Cooke, the agent for Matson Navigation Co., would set the schedule and passenger list. Castle & Cooke would notify the newspapers and a reporter friend would invariably call Baker. He loved to take his camera down to the dock to photograph the ships and any important people aboard.

As the ship rounded Diamond Head small boats filled with hotel representatives, newspaper reporters, photographers and health officials would meet the ship. While the hotel people made room assignments, the news people ran up and down the decks of the vessel looking for the passengers they wanted to interview. Presorted ship's mail returned on the small boats and was taken immediately to the Honolulu postoffice.

Mailbags were left hanging at the foot of the gangplank of the departing ship for the deposit of last-minute correspondence. Sometimes mail boys would race to the pier just as the ship left its moorings and pulled away. They would toss packets of letters to the laughing passengers on deck.

As the ship left its mooring the Royal Hawaiian Band usually played *Aloha Oe*, or *Farewell to Thee* while it steamed out of the harbor. Friends of the passengers would then jump in their automobiles and race around to the Diamond Head Lighthouse. Here they got a final glimpse of the ship before it disappeared around Koko Head.

Following the attack on Pearl Harbor, the Matson Navigation Company's passenger liners were confiscated by the U.S. Government and became troop ships. They were returned to civilian service after the war but by the mid-1950's the airplane had taken over as the primary means of travel between California and the Hawaiian Islands. Boat Days were never quite the same again.

Two ships tied up at Alakea Street Wharf, Pier 7, 1914

Boat Day, Alakea Street Wharf Pier 7, 1914

Empress of Canada — **Canadian-Australian Line, 1932**

President Taft, **Dollar Line, 1932**

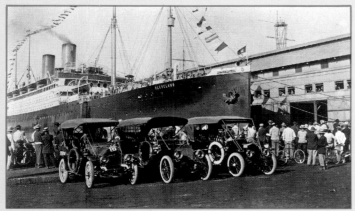

President Cleveland, **Dollar Line, 1914**

Tusitala, 1931

Crowds going to see friends off, 1936

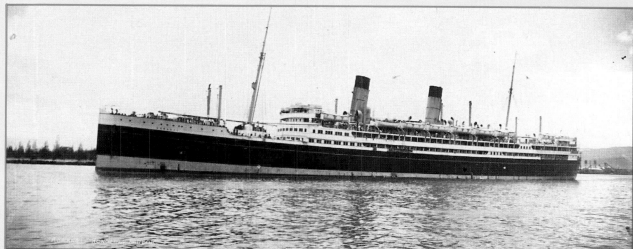

Aorangi, Canadian-Australian Line, 1932

Tenyu Maru, N.Y.K. Line, 1932

Cars parked near Alakea Street Wharf. In rear are the coal yards used for fuel for the ships. 1914

A ship's Hawaiian Orchestra, 1914

Matson Liner, *Matsonia*, leaving Honolulu, 1932

1 Typical colorful lei bedecked passenger, 1926

2 Baker filming the departure of author Christopher Morley, 1934

3 Afternoon tea on the promenade deck, 1912

4 The multicolored leis of boat day, 1932

City of Los Angeles, Los Angeles Steamship Co., 1929

Boat day children with a catch of crabs at the dock, 1930

Alexander Hume Ford, departing for the Orient in 1924

City of Los Angeles, Los Angeles Steamship Co., 1926

A ship's captain, 1912

The many modes of transportation on boat day. Horses and carriages, the trolley cars and automobiles, 1912

Boys diving for coins tossed over the side by tourists, 1924

Police supervising boat day traffic, 1936

A Matson liner in port, 1932

Asama Maru, N.Y.K. Line, 1930

President Hayes, 1932

Empress of Britain, Canadian-Australasian Line, 1932

Chichibu Muru, N.Y.K. Line, 1934

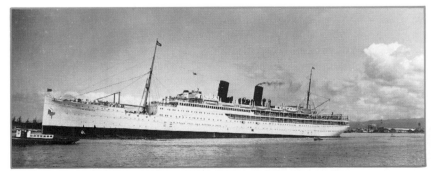

City of Honolulu, Los Angeles Steamship Co., 1926

President Hoover, $ Dollar Line, 1932

Passengers disembarking, Honolulu, 1935

Christopher Columbus, 1932

President Polk, $ Dollar Line, 1932

Mariposa, Matson Navigation Co., 1934

Waikiki Beach and surf in front of the Outrigger Canoe Club, 1916

Passenger ships were arriving regularly from the
mainland and Waikiki was well on its way to
becoming the most famous stretch
of beach in the world.

WAIKIKI

By 1908, the year that Ray Jerome Baker arrived in Hawaii, tourism in the islands was beginning to flower. Passenger ships were arriving regularly from the mainland and Waikiki was well on its way to becoming the most famous stretch of beach in the world.

The name Waikiki is usually translated as "spouting water," a reference to the natural springs which used to keep the area wet year-round. At the turn of the century there were 15 surveyed duck and fishponds in the area with several interior ponds turned into rice paddies and taro patches. During heavy rains the Manoa and Palolo Streams tended to overflow and there was widespread flooding.

There were about a hundred cars on Oahu at this time but the most popular means of transportation from downtown Honolulu to Waikiki was by electric streetcar. It cost a nickel to make the three-mile trip.

Most visitors stayed at the Moana, the first of the Waikiki's deluxe resort hotels, which had opened in 1901 with 75 guest rooms. A wooden pier, which Baker often photographed, extended 300-feet onward into the ocean.

Nearby was Kapiolani Park which had been given to the people of Hawaii by King Kalakaua in 1877 and named after his Queen. Here, alongside the shadow of Diamond Head, spectators could watch horse racing, polo and starlight concerts by the Royal Hawaiian Band.

Waikiki in the early days fascinated Baker. He returned time and time again to take photographs around the hotels and beaches. In September of 1911, Baker and his wife, Edith, rented a cottage on Beach Road and later purchased a house and land at 1911 Kalakaua Avenue. The sign over the front door, long a familiar sight in Waikiki, read "R.J. Baker, Photographer, Publisher of Fine Books, Moving Pictures, Lantern Slides."

The Royal Hawaiian Hotel opened in 1927 with a party for 1,200 guests. In the late 20's and early 30's the hotel was frequented by movie stars and millionaires. Even in the depression years the "Pink Castle" remained a first-class resort.

Baker's photography business proved highly profitable through the 1920's but by the middle 1930's the profits started to lag. Fortunately, he had acquired adjoining properties in 1926 and 1936 and he was soon renting out apartments at prices ranging from $25 to $40 per month.

His studio was a busy place during World War II and he worked day and night meeting the demands of servicemen who wanted their pictures taken before they went overseas to an uncertain fate. After the war these servicemen went home and Baker's studio grew dark again. He seldom took photographs in Waikiki after 1950, preferring his memory of its charming past to the reality of its commercial present.

Moana and Royal Hawaiian hotels, 1929

Ray Jerome Baker carefully posed Diamond Head in the background when he took the above photograph of the Moana and Royal Hawaiian hotels.

The Moana, which opened in 1901, was the first grand resort hotel in Waikiki. In 1927, two years before this picture was taken, she was joined by the Royal Hawaiian which was built on the site where Queen Kaahumanu once had her summer home.

The Halekulani Hotel began in 1907 as The Hau Tree Inn. Ten years later it was christened the Halekulani, a name that translates to "House Befitting Heaven." Baker was a frequent visitor to all three hotels, especially the Halekulani where he often ate lunch in its ocean-side Hau Tree Lanai.

The Moana Hotel from the lawn of the Moana Cottages, 1924. This grassy area became the Princess Kaiulani Hotel in 1955.

Main Building of the Halekulani Hotel, 1936

Hau Tree Lanai of the Halekulani Hotel, 1920

The Dining Room of the Halekulani Hotel, 1930

Diamond Head and the Royal Hawaiian and Moana hotels, 1929

Outrigger canoe and surfers at Waikiki, 1932

Main drive at Fort DeRussy, 1918

Waikiki rice fields, looking toward Diamond Head from the McCully area. Negative "enhanced" by Norman Hill to include moonlight, 1914

Punchbowl from the future Ala Moana Center, 1908

The Ala Wai looking toward St. Louis Heights from the bridge along Ala Moana Boulevard. Aloha Motors is on the left, 1948

Residence of Bertha Young and the Royal Hawaiian Hotel, 1928

Aerial view of the Royal Hawaiian Hotel and the Moana Hotel and pier at Waikiki, 1933

Outrigger canoe sails off Diamond Head, 1908

Lighthouse at Diamond Head, 1914

Famous beach boys and surfers, 1914

Sans Souci Beach looking toward the McInerny residence from in front of the War Memorial Natatorium, 1926

Kaiulani Street. To the left are the Moana Cottages, and on the right the residence of Mrs. Fullard-Leo, 1940

Outrigger Canoe Club, the Moana Hotel and its pier, 1924

Playing in the surf, Waikiki, 1918

Royal Hawaiian Glee Club, 1928

Surfer and dog riding the waves at Waikiki, 1932

Kodak Hula Show, 1937

Near Makee Island, 1910, an area which now is occupied by the Waikiki Shell and the Honolulu Zoo.

Rows of coconut trees near Sans Souci Beach, Waikiki, 1928

Moana Hotel, 1920

Kalakaua Avenue at the beginning of Kapiolani Park, 1915

Children along Hobron Lane, 1935

Looking mauka, this area is today occupied by the Waipuna, along John Ena Road and Hobron Lane, 1932

Canal Cafe, 1932

Cottages along Hobron Lane, 1935

Daisy

Daisy, the Honolulu Zoo's African elephant, came to Honolulu in 1916 aboard a ship bound for the mainland. She was bought by money raised by the city's school children and for the next two decades she was the zoo's star attraction.

Over the years, however, Daisy grew quite temperamental. On March 3, 1933, she trampled to death her keeper and was immediately killed by police officers. Her body was then towed out to sea and left behind for the sharks.

Daisy the Honolulu Zoo elephant, 1921

A peacock on the grounds of the estate of Governor Cleghorn and his beloved daughter Princess Victoria Kaiulani, Waikiki, 1908

Surfing at Waikiki, 1918

A lady surfer, tennis shoes and all, and a
cheese cake pose, 1918

Paddling a canoe in front of the Outrigger Canoe Club, and the Moana Hotel. A view taken from the front of the Seaside Hotel which was the site of the Royal Hawaiian, 1922

Along the corner of Ala Moana Boulevard and Hobron Lane, 1935

South Seas Restaurant and Night Club at the junction of McCully Street and Kalakaua Avenue. 1932

Warriors landing from invasion fleet, Waikiki, 1910

1910 Commemorative Pageant

On February 22, 1906, thirty automobiles decorated in every manner possible, along with private carriages, decorated bicycles, cowboys on horseback and fifty ladies who were to revive the old pa'u riding of the past, assembled in what became the beginning of Hawaii's famed parades.

By 1907, pretty girls were introduced as Princesses of the parade, as well as theme floats. Luaus and numerous athletic events marked the afternoon's events, and a street carnival was held in the evening.

In 1910 a pageant was added to commemorate the 115th anniversary of the landing of Kamehameha the Great. Here, at a location in front of the old Outrigger Canoe Club and to the Diamond Head side of the Seaside Hotel, a great flotilla of forty canoes arrived filled with soldiers carrying kahilis and spears. Shortly thereafter on the horizon there appeared the great war canoe carrying Kamehameha the Great. Amid ceremonies of tribute, homage was paid to the great warrior chief led by Madame Pauahi, famed hula dancer of the court of King Kalakaua. This marked the first public display of hula in years.

The hula troop and the warriors all sweltered beneath union suits dyed brown to symbolize Hawaiian skin, for Hawaii was in the midst of a morality consciousness started by the Reverend Stephen Desha of the Haili Church in Hilo "It was immoral to show your bare skin on the beach at Waikiki."

The performance was repeated in 1913.

In 1914 the event was re-christened the Mid-Pacific Carnival and held over a ten-day period.

In 1916 the event became the Kamehameha Day parade, even though there was still a continued outcry over the exhibitioning of the "evil hula."

The kahili bearers mark the arrival of Kamehameha, 1910

Kamehameha arrives flanked by his attendants and a large retinue of spear carrying guards

Kamehameha and his attendants, 1910

Warriors and court hula dancers assembled on the beach shortly after the arrival of Kamehameha, February 22, 1910

Dancers of the Court of Kamehameha, Pageant at Waikiki, 1910

Chanters, 1910

The royal dancers pay tribute to Kamehameha, 1910

Looking up Kalakaua Avenue towards the Waikiki Tavern, 1949

Shops and apartments alongside the Waikiki Tavern, 1949

Waikiki Tavern and shops, 1949

Part of the Waikiki Tavern complex with buildings designed by Shadinger, 1949

James Steiner residence and the Waikiki Bowling Alley, 1949

Waikiki Bowling Alley, next to the James Steiner residence, 1949

Waikiki Bowling Alley, Waikiki Beach Grocery and the Hustace family residence, 1949

Hustace residence, 1949, torn down to make way for the Surfrider Hotel. The Moana Hotel is in the distance

Baker spent several months on the plantation
of the Oahu Sugar Co. in Waipahu
photographing in the fields and factory.

AGRICULTURE

Most of Ray Jerome Baker's early Hawaiian photographs were either landscapes, buildings or portraits of the Hawaiian people themselves. Later he developed an interest in the activities of other ethnic groups.

In 1936 he was contacted by Ward Bowen, director of the Visual Instruction Division of the University of the State of New York. Bowen asked him to make a series of photographs for the University that would illustrate the growing, cultivation and harvesting of sugar cane as well as the manufacture of raw sugar.

Baker spent several months on the plantation of the Oahu Sugar Co. in Waipahu photographing in the fields and factory. His camera captured the labors of the Chinese, Japanese, Portuguese and Filipino workers.

Although sugar cane was among the crops brought to Hawaii by the first Polynesian settlers, its farming continued on a small scale until the middle of the 19th century when increased technology and expanding markets made it a profitable business. In 1876, the Treaty of Reciprocity eliminated the heavy tariff on Hawaiian sugar entering U.S. ports.

The real key to developing a strong sugar industry, however, was the building of a large labor force. Organized importation of Chinese laborers began in 1852 followed by the importation of Japanese and Portuguese workers in 1868 and 1878. Finally, in 1906, the first Filipino group arrived.

Out in the fields, Baker found that Hawaii's imported ethnic groups were dependable workers. They cleared new lands by cutting away trees and brush and plowed the earth with their teams of horses. They then planted, fertilized and irrigated the fields. At harvest time they burned the fields to remove the undergrowth, used their machetes to cut the juicy stalks and loaded them into flat-bed cars bound for the mills.

Down at the factory more workers unloaded the cars, operated the cleaning and crushing machines, and fed the furnaces that boiled the juice away into molasses and sugar crystals. Finally they packed the individual bags of sugar for shipment.

After the resulting photographs were sent to the University, Baker decided to publish a limited edition book, *The Romance of Raw Sugar*, which contained over 70 actual photographs as the illustrations. The text was written by William Wolters, an agricultural consultant for the Waipahu mill. Baker made up 25 copies of the book and priced them at $27.50 each.

Savoring the success of *The Romance of Raw Sugar*, Baker took additional documentary photographs of Hawaii's pineapple, rice and cattle industries. While most were never published in book form they remain today a valuable historical record of commercial agriculture in Hawaii.

Deep plowing machine, Ewa Plantation, 1930

Women in the field, 1908

Sugar cane along an irrigation ditch, 1916

Sugar cane in tassel, 1916

Cutting sugar cane on Maui, 1915

Plantation workers wait for the train, Oahu, 1924

Workers cutting sugar cane, 1916

Plantation worker on a lunch break, Maui, 1915

Mother and baby in the field, 1918

Loading the cut sugar cane onto flat cars for transportation
to the mill, 1918

Plantation children, 1930

Loading the cut sugar cane onto flat cars for transportation to the mill, 1930

Cut sugar cane on the way to the mill, 1918

Chinese granite crushing stones, Koloa Plantation, Kauai, 1915

Chinese granite crushing stones and the Koloa Plantation train, Koloa, Kauai, 1915

In the boiling room at the mill, 1918

Vaccum pan, Oahu Sugar Co., 1922

Plantation houses, 1926

Plantation kindergarten, 1922

Plantation workers in a pineapple field, Maui, 1922

Rows of pineapple, Oahu, 1924

Plantation workers plant rows of pineapple between mulch paper, 1926

Rows of pineapple, Oahu, 1924

Rows of pineapple, Oahu, 1928

Pineapple plant, 1924

Trail and Mountain Club members pose by the road during a hike to the pineapple fields, 1924

Packing pineapple in the fields, 1924

Dole Pineapple Co. advertisement, 1914

Dole Pineapple Co., Honolulu, 1928

Planting rice, Pearl City, Oahu, 1917

Plowing rice fields with a water buffalo, Pearl City, Oahu, 1917

Plowing rice fields with a water buffalo, Pearl City, Oahu, 1917

Farmer plows the rice field with oxen, Oahu, 1924

Rice fields, banana and mango trees, Kaneohe, Oahu, 1922

Planting rice, Pearl City, Oahu, 1914

Harvesting rice, Kahuku, Oahu, 1926

Plowing rice fields with a pair of water buffalo, Kaneohe, Oahu, 1917

Harvesting taro, Waiahole, Oahu, 1926

Duck ponds and taro in the McCully district, Honolulu, 1918

Rice farmer with water buffalo, Pearl City, 1918

Riding the cattle range at Parker Ranch, Hawaii, 1918

Cattle on the range at Parker Ranch, Hawaii, 1918

Loading sheep at Niihau, 1908

Rowing the cattle out to the boat, Kawaihae, Hawaii, 1918

Loading cattle aboard a boat, Kawaihae, Hawaii, 1918

Sheep herding at Parker Ranch, Hawaii, 1935

Riding out to a boat to load cattle at Kawaihae, Hawaii, 1926

Tying cattle to the side of the boats at Kawaihae, Hawaii, 1926

Rowing cattle out to the Humuula to be shipped to Honolulu, Kawaihae, Hawaii, 1926

It was Baker's habit for many years to take a photographic inventory of downtown Honolulu.

Corner of Fort and King Streets. Hobron Drug Co., 1908

OLD HAWAII

Sometime during his first decade in Hawaii, Ray Jerome Baker became interested in the architecture of Honolulu. Whenever he photographed a building he would go inside and ask the occupants about its history. He inquired about the date it was built, previous owners and any other facts worth knowing.

Writing in 1955, Baker recalled that "when I first came to Honolulu with my wife in 1908, it was almost like the country. The streets were not lighted very well, and there was little going on at night."

He remembered that there were rice paddies on the grounds of present-day McKinley High School and that most of the area between McCully Street and Kalakaua Avenue was swampland or occupied by duck ponds and banana fields. The Ala Wai Canal, along which he would stroll frequently in later life, still hadn't been built.

"Now there are 24-hour filling stations," he continued, "and eating places, and I guess some of the night clubs make whoopee until morning. (I wouldn't know, because I do not frequent such places.) We have neon lights, parking problems, door to door salesmen, juvenile delinquency and most of the other ??? blessings of civilization."

It was Baker's habit for many years to take a photographic inventory of downtown Honolulu. Usually on January 2 he would park his car near the Kamehameha statue and walk along King Street to Palama and over to the Kaumakapili Church. Then he'd turn around and walk back on Beretania to South Street and over again to King.

During his trip he'd photograph new buildings and other sights that caught his eye. He took similar hikes through Waikiki, starting along Kalakaua Avenue and winding his way up and down the many sidestreets. In the early days people were accustomed to seeing Baker carrying around his camera and he made friends easily. Whenever they saw him they'd wave from their porches or stop on the street to talk.

In November, 1941, just a month before the bombing of Pearl Harbor, Baker printed *Honolulu Then and Now*, a book he subtitled "a photographic record of progress in the City of Honolulu." In addition to his own photos he included many that were taken by others before him.

"The easy going, leisurely way of life…has gone forever," he wrote in the book's Foreword. No longer excited about documenting the present, he chose instead to publish his favorite pictures from the past. "Many strangers have come," he wrote with regret, "and the old timer who walks the downtown streets of Honolulu may do so without meeting a single person he knows."

Looking down Fort Street from the front of Liberty House, 1927

Honolulu automobile stand on Hotel Street near Bishop, 1910

Corner of Fort and Hotel streets with Benson Smith on the left and Liberty House, H. F. Wichman and Curtis, Ltd., on the right. Detor Jewelers is on the corner, 1922

Front of the Alexander Young Hotel building decorated for July 4th, 1917

Trolley coming up Fort Street to corner of Hotel, 1922.

Fair Department Store and the Central Fire Station at Beretania and Fort Streets, 1916

Lewers and Cooke Lumber Yard, corner of Queen and Punchbowl streets, 1910. Later Moe Lipton's Auction Room. It was torn down to build the Department of Transportation.

Looking up Kaahumanu Street towards the old Merchant Street Post Office, 1908

Central YMCA at the corner of Hotel and Alakea streets. Up the street is the Mutual Telephone Co., 1937

The Ladies Lounge facing Fort Street in The Liberty House, 1919

B. F. Ehlers and Co. (later Liberty House) decorated for Washington's Birthday, 1908

The Dry Goods Department of The Liberty House, Fort Street, 1919.

Iolani Palace, 1922

Banyan tree to the rear of Iolani Palace, 1922

Kawaiahao Church, 1940

Alexander and Baldwin, 1933

Alexander Young Hotel Building, 1908

Looking toward the Alexander Young Hotel, 1924

Looking toward the Young Hotel, from the roof of the Stangenwald Building, 1914

Alexander Young Hotel in 1917. Bishop Street had not yet been cut through at Hotel Street.

Looking down Bishop Street from the block just above Hotel Street. The building at the left was the old Steiner-Hart Building. At this corner, the Spence-Cliff Restaurant chain had their start, 1940

Masonic Temple at the corner of Hotel and Alakea streets, 1916

McCandless Building. Bethel and King streets, 1908

Hub Clothiers at Fort and Hotel streets, 1940

Corner of Beretania and Alakea streets, 1920

E.O. Hall and Sons, at the corner of
Fort and King streets, 1916

Upper Fort Street looking down towards Princess Theatre,
1945. This area in later years was the site of Kukui Plaza.

The Honolulu Advertiser and radio station KGU. To the left is
the Crystal Market, 1936

Looking toward Kaimuki and Diamond Head from the roof of
Honolulu Hale, the City Hall, 1936

The Sachs Block, the Leonard Hotel and Jeff's Fashion Company and the Princess Theater at Fort and Beretania Street, 1924. Today it is the site of Kukui Plaza, 1982

Central Fire Station, upper corner of Fort and Beretania Streets, 1916

Kamehameha the Great, 1922

Mediterranean Court, Honolulu
Academy of Arts, 1934

Looking down Nuuanu Street from Judd,
1908

Corner of Fort and Beretania, 1924

Junction of King and Bishop streets, 1935

Looking down Bishop Street from the roof of the Alexander Young Hotel, showing Bishop Park, Bank of Hawaii, Bishop Trust Co. and Alexander and Baldwin, 1940

The Blaisdell Hotel, Fort Street at Chaplain Lane, 1926

Honolulu Fire Department shows off the old and the new equipment in a parade, at the corner of Beretania and Alapai Street, May 1, 1921

Ray Jerome Baker took this photograph of the Mission Frame House, above left, and the Printing House, right, in 1930. The Frame House is the oldest known wooden building in the Hawaiian Islands, also the oldest wooden building west of the Mississippi River.

Mission House

Seven men, their wives and five children arrived in Kailua, Kona, aboard the brig *Thaddeus* on April 4, 1820. These were the first Christian missionaries to Hawaii and had been sent to the Islands from Boston by the American Board of Commissioners for Foreign Missions.

Only two men in this pioneer company were ordained ministers. One was Asa Thurston, who remained in Kona, and the other was Hiram Bingham, who sailed on to Honolulu. The remaining male members of the group included a doctor, a printer, a farmer and two teachers. All of them were under forty. Bingham and Thurston were barely in their thirties and the oldest, Daniel Chamberlain, a farmer with five children, was thirty-seven.

The two-story Frame House was erected in 1821 with prefabricated materials shipped to Honolulu around Cape Horn from Boston. The missionaries added locally salvaged lumber to the original wood and lined the cellar walls with adobe made from thick mud mixed with straw.

As soon as the Frame House was built, Daniel Chamberlain and his family moved into the first finished room. Part of the cellar was used as a dining room while the cooking was done in a little stone-and-mud house nearby.

The small, two-roomed coral building is known as the Printing House and contains a replica of the original Rampage press brought to the Islands by the missionaries in 1820. The first printing west of the Mississippi was done in this building.

Washington Place is the oldest house in Hawaii continuously used as a residence. The style of this two-story, 17-room structure is of Greek Revival architecture.

Ten of Hawaii's fourteen governors have lived here as well as one Governor of Oahu when Hawaii was still a kingdom. Washington Place was also home to Queen Liliuokalani, the last of Hawaii's reigning monarchs.

This beautiful house was built over a four-year period, 1842-1846, by Isaac Hart, a master mechanic hired by John Dominis, an American sea captain. Dominis had come from New York with his wife and young son to live in Honolulu.

Dominis was lost at sea soon after the building was completed. His son, John Owen Dominis, grew up to become an important government leader in the kingdom and, in 1862, married the honorable Lydia K. P. Kapaakea, sister of Chief David Kalakaua. Dominis was then named the Governor of Oahu by King Kamehameha V.

After David Kalakaua became king in 1874, his brother Leleiohoku became the heir apparent. Upon Leleiohoku's death their sister became the heir apparent under the title of Princess Liliuokalani. She became Queen Liliuokalani after Kalakaua's death in 1891.

Dominis was given the title Prince Consort but, unfortunately, died seven months after his wife came to the throne. She inherited Washington Place and moved there from her royal quarters at Iolani Palace after the overthrow of the monarchy in 1893.

Queen Liliuokalani died at Washington Place on November 11, 1917, at the age of seventy-nine. In 1922 her home became the official residence of Hawaii's governors.

Washington Place, 1932

Washington Place

J.B. Castle residence, Waikiki, 1916

Princess Ruth's old home Keoua Hale, 1908

Princess Ruth's old home as Central Grammar School, 1924

Haleiwa Hotel, Haleiwa, Oahu, 1910

Residence of Doris Duke Cromwell, 1938

Residence of Claus Spreckels, Punahou Street, Honolulu, 1908

Sampans built in the Funai Boat Yards at the Ward Estate, 1926

The lagoon at the Old Plantation, 1916

Lagoon at the Old Plantation, 1916

Entrance to the Old Plantation, King Street, 1916

Victoria Robinson Ward and her husband, Curtis Perry Ward, built their large two and one-half story home, "Old Plantation," on a portion of some thirty acres of land bounded by what would eventually be Ward Avenue, South King Street, and Kapiolani Boulevard. Completed in 1880, this colonial styled mansion had its stables and carriage house and its own school house for the children of the household. It was soon surrounded by lush gardens, thousands of cocopalms, and a windmill to pump water for irrigation throughout the grounds. As well, there was a large boating lagoon with a teahouse on its makai border. The pond itself was well stocked with the finest varieties of Hawaiian fish

In 1910, Ray Jerome Baker became a friend of Mrs. Ward and her daughters, and frequently was a guest at the "Old Plantation." Upon the publication of the song, "Old Plantation," Mr. Baker took many of his fine photographs of the Ward Estate to illustrate the sheet music.

Hawaiian pau riders leaving the Ward Estate, The Old Plantation, 1912

"Old Plantation"

Boating on the lagoon at the Old Plantation, 1916

Chinese duck farm near Sheridan and Kapiolani Boulevard, 1908

Corner of Pensacola and Kapiolani Boulevard, 1940

Atkinson Drive and Kapiolani Boulevard, 1946

Pearl City

Pearl City, Oahu, had been created as the end of the line for the Oahu Railway by 1889. Here Benjamin F. Dillingham subdivided and sold lots on a peninsula of land which bordered on the East Lock of Pearl Harbor Lagoon. To its upper borders were thousands of acres of rice fields operated by enterprising Chinese farmers. At the railway depot a four-horse team and wagon took passengers down a road to various residences of kamaaina Honoluluans.

With the advent of World War II, all of this land was condemned and reclaimed by the U.S. Government.

Rice fields near Pearl City, Oahu, 1916

Overlooking Pearl Harbor, 1916

The fleet, Pearl Harbor, Oahu, 1940

Aiea Mill overlooking Pearl Harbor, 1922

Walter Dillingham explains the layout of Pearl Harbor and the dredging of
Honolulu Harbor, 1910

Chinese Temple, Lahaina, Maui, 1908

Taro growing near Waihee, Maui, 1912

Pioneer Hotel, Lahaina, Maui, 1922

Along the waterfront, Lahaina, Maui, 1912

Hawaiian Airlines landing in Kailua-Kona, 1936

Bridge along the Hilo Railway, Hawaii, 1918

Along the waterfront of Kailua-Kona, the view from Hulihee Palace, 1926

Court House, Kailua-Kona, 1959

The main lanai of the Kona Inn, 1934

Bathing beauties at the salt water pool of the Kona Inn, Kailua-Kona, 1934

Along the waterfront, Kailua-Kona, 1912

L. Chong Store, Pahala, Hawaii, 1924

Hakalau Plantation Mill, Hakalau, Hawaii, 1924

The entrance to Moanalua Gardens, 1914

Moanalua Gardens

Moanalua Gardens is a privately owned park maintained by the Damon Estate. When Samuel Mills Damon died in 1924, his will provided that the lands be retained for the enjoyment of the public.

Damon, a business and governmental leader and owner of the Bishop Bank, now called First Hawaiian, had purchased some of the land himself and inherited the rest from Princess Bernice Pauahi Bishop upon her death in 1884. He began developing it soon afterwards.

On a trip to Great Britain in 1897 to represent the Republic of Hawaii at the Diamond Jubilee of Queen Victoria, Damon visited the Edinburgh University botany department and Kew Garden. There he met a young graduate, 26-year-old Donald Mcintyre, and asked him to return to Hawaii as his head gardener.

Macintyre turned the Moanalua Gardens into a place of exceptional beauty. He built a large orchid collection and imported plants such as the anthurium and the bird of paradise. Choice fruits, such as the banana, mango and papaya, were also grown in abundance.

The Japanese Garden at Moanalua was one of Hawaii's showcases before it was discontinued after World War I. It contained a teahouse modeled after one in Kyoto, bridges over streams, waterfalls, stone lanterns, and classically clipped trees.

When Ray Jerome Baker took the photographs on these pages, Moanalua Gardens was at the heights of its glory. While distinguished visitors were entertained in the main house, others drove out in automobiles or rode the streetcar to the end of the line at Fort Shafter and took their lunch under the spreading monkeypod trees.

In the Japanese Garden, Moanalua Gardens, 1914

In Moanalua Gardens, 1918

The Chinese garden near Shafter Flats, 1914

An auwai in Moanalua Gardens, 1914

Oahu Railroad Depot, King and Iwilei streets, 1916

The Railroad Depot at Waianae, Oahu, 1918

Oahu Sugar Company Mill at Waipahu, Oahu, with rice field in the foreground as seen from an Oahu railway train, 1922

Scenery along the Oahu Railway in the area between Pearl City and Waiau, Oahu, 1916

Lau Yee Chai was said at the time to be the most beautiful Chinese restaurant in the world. It was located at the beginning of Kuhio Avenue and the junction of Kalakaua Avenue on the spot now occupied by the Ambassador Hotel. The main entrance is seen in the upper photograph (1930). "Me P.Y. Chong," the famed host and owner, is in the lower photograph smiling as usual. (1930)

An inner garden court pool, 1930

The cashier and cigar and cigarette counter, 1930

Baker thought nothing of taking his camera and
disappearing for days in Hawaii's
wilderness areas.

Hanauma Bay, 1920

SCENIC WONDERS

"Every year," wrote Alexander Hume Ford in an early issue of his *Mid-Pacific Magazine,* some artist or mainland photographer known to fame visits Hawaii and carries away bits of tropical scenery that the rest of the world may enjoy. The best of these artists in a photographic way to visit Hawaii is Ray Jerome Baker."

Mid-Pacific Magazine was a monthly journal published and edited by Ford in Honolulu. He went on to say that Baker had begun to make Hawaii his home and that his pictures would thereafter appear regularly in the magazine. The young photographer was thus assured of a wide audience for his work.

Baker was an experienced hiker and he thought nothing of taking his camera and disappearing for days in Hawaii's wilderness areas. He crossed countless mountains and valleys searching for the perfect landscape shot. Once, during a trip to Lanai, a strong gust of wind blew his equipment over the side of a cliff and, according to Ford, "hurled it bounding down a thousand feet along the rocky edges."

Because it was his only large-format camera, Baker climbed over the face of the cliff and carefully inched his way to the bottom. He located all of the broken parts and later reassembled them in Honolulu. At other times he returned from a trip only to find that his camera had malfunctioned or that sheets of film had been badly damaged by heat and moisture.

Although he was temperamentally a loner, Baker joined the Hawaiian Trail and Mountain Club in 1921 and was an officer and director for many years. He even wrote the club's unpublished history. Founded by Ford a decade before, the organization had a clubhouse in Waimanalo and sponsored regular trips around the Islands.

"Personally," explained Baker during a June 1937 radio broadcast, "I do not enjoy the real long hikes. I like to go leisurely and visit with my companions or study the plant life, the geology of the region or the land shells, birds and insects."

In April of the following year he spent several weeks camping on the Big Island. He took scenic photographs as he hiked around its volcano country, forests and beaches. A few months later he published a book of 130 photographs, most of which were taken during this trip. It was entitled *Hawaii, Isle of a Thousand Wonders.*

Ford, in the same *Mid-Pacific Magazine* story quoted above, referred to Baker as the "pioneer" who made the Islands "known to the world with his camera." He concluded by noting "there is more varied scenery in Hawaii than is to be found in any equal area of earth's surface, and Hawaii is fortunate in having Ray Jerome Baker awakened to this fact."

Along the beach near the Natatorium, 1928

Coastline near Halawa Valley, Molokai, 1920

Diamond Head from Tantalus, 1922

Sunset off of Waikiki, 1916

Scenic ocean and rock along Waianae Coast, 1918

Coast near Kaena Point, 1918

Coastline near Waianae, 1920

Sunset near Pearl City, 1916

Nuuanu Pali, Oahu, 1912

Looking over the Koolau Range with Diamond Head in the distance, 1933

Sacred Falls, Oahu, 1918

Scenic valley near Sacred Falls, Oahu, 1918

Water buffalo grazing in field near
Hygenic Dairy, Heeia, Oahu, 1922

Swamp lands, Kaneohe, 1918

Koolau Range near Kaneohe, 1918

Mount Olomana peak, 1933

Banana and rice fields, Kaneohe, 1920

Rice fields, Kaneohe, 1920. Koolau Range in background

Sunset on Kaneohe Bay, 1920

Sunset, Coconut Island, Kaneohe Bay, 1916

Island between Kailua and Lanikai, 1933

Lahaina looking toward Molokai, 1918

Molokai from Lahaina, 1912

Near Lahaina, Maui 1908

Lahaina, Maui, 1908

Sunset over Lanai, from Lahaina, 1908

Sunset near Olowalu, 1908

Interior, Haleakala, 1914

Coastline beyond Lahaina, Maui, 1921

Wailuku, Maui, 1908

Maui plantation town, 1923

Hanalei Valley, 1914

Rice paddies near Kilauea, Kauai, 1912

Hanalei Bay, 1912

Napali Coast, 1912

Waimea Canyon, 1914

Waterfall, Hamakua Coast, Hawaii, 1914

Railroad along the Hamakua Coast, Hawaii, 1918

Hibiscus, *Hibiscus tiliaceus*, Linnaeus

Baker was a frequent visitor to Foster Botanic
Gardens and often took photographs there to
illustrate his talks on Island plants.

FRUITS AND FLOWERS

Ray Jerome Baker had a personal library of over 700 books. Although he enjoyed reading the classics, little of this was fiction. Most of his collection consisted of works on history, photography and the natural sciences.

One of his favorite volumes was William Hillebrand's *Flora of the Hawaiian Islands*, published in 1888 and regarded by Baker as the "local botanist's Bible." The book was long out of print and the photographer valued the copy he had.

Hillebrand was a German physician who came to Hawaii in 1850 and became the first director of Queen's Hospital. Later he also served as Commissioner of Immigration and travelled widely in this capacity. In 1855, Queen Kalama, the widow of Kamehameha III, sold Hillebrand several acres of property on the outskirts of Honolulu. Here, in the gardens surrounding his home, he introduced many species of plants which he was to collect during his travels.

Upon his return to Germany in 1867, Hillebrand sold his beautiful home to Captain and Mrs. Thomas Foster who continued to develop the acreage by adding even more ornamental trees, shrubs and flowers. Mrs. Foster, a sister of Victoria Ward, bequeathed Foster Botanic Gardens to Honolulu in 1930 as a city park.

After its opening to the public, Baker was a frequent visitor to Foster Botanic Gardens and often took photographs there to illustrate his talks on Island plants. He also took slow-motion films of flowers opening their petals and sometimes projected these at his lectures. One of his most popular talks was "Native and Ornamental Plants of Hawaii."

Flowers which normally took an entire day to open and close did so on Baker's screen in 30 seconds. "In some cases we clip the petals away from the flower, leaving the pistil exposed. The opening of the pollen sacks and the shedding of the pollen, which resembles bunches of grapes, due to the fact that this scene is taken through a microscope, makes an extremely interesting detail."

In 1937, responding to numerous requests that he present his plant photographs in book form, he published *Familiar Hawaiian Flowers* which consisted of original black-and-white pictures meticulously hand-colored by his wife. Edith Baker, although not trained in art, developed into a skilled photographic colorist. She was a patient artist who enjoyed spending hours painting the leaves and blooms of her husband's photographs.

The book came in two sizes, one of 150 photos and another of 54. The fly-leaves carried the name of the native plant or flower, the botanical name and usually a brief description. Baker dedicated the book to "the pioneer botanists who, unaided by the act of photography, first revealed the richness and beauty of the flora in these islands." Following in their footsteps he felt proud to have added to their heritage.

Strawberry guava, *Psidium guajava*, **Linnaeus**

Lemon guava, *Psidium guajava*, **Linnaeus**

Guava, *Psidium guajava*, **Linnaeus**

Vegetables of the Hawaii garden: sugar cane, radishes, cabbage, carrots, yams, lotus, taro, tomato, peppers and onions

Coffee beans

Guava, Lemon guava
(Psidium guajava, Linnaeus)
The fruit is packed with a mildly acid, pleasant-tasting pulp in which are embedded numerous hard seeds. The shrub or tree, twenty or more feet in height, grows wild. Superficially the guava resembles the lemon, but the interior is quite different. The fruit is collected chiefly for jam and jelly making.

Papaya, pineapple, bananas, mangoes and avocado

Pomelo, grapefruit, kona oranges, tangerine and limes

Breadfruit, Ulu
(Artocarpus incisa, Linnaeus)
Breadfruit was never very extensively used for food in Hawaii, but native people in other islands of the Pacific considered it formed an important article of diet. There are a number of varieties, some having attractive, deeply indented foliage, while on others the leaves are nearly entire. The male flowers grow separately, though on the same tree with the female, and when ripe the fruit is brown. The fruit is seldom more than six inches in diameter, filled with mealy, white to deep yellow pulp and is usually prepared by baking. The tree grows thirty to forty feet tall.

Banana
(Musa sapientum, Linnaeus)
Within the turn of the present century bananas have become one of the best-known fruits in the world. Improved transportation has changed its status from that of an almost exclusively tropical fruit to one distributed almost everywhere in the temperate zones. Bananas grow in clusters consisting of a dozen to fifteen members and known as "hands." Each stalk bears but one bunch of fruit and a year or more is required for its development. After maturity the old stalk may be cut down and new ones develop from the same roots. There are nearly forty varieties of bananas listed as growing in Hawaii. It is believed that bananas were introduced by the early Hawaiians and used extensively for food by them. Today there are many wild bananas growing in the Hawaiian mountains.

Breadfruit, *Artocarpus incisa,* **Linnaeus**

Mulberry

Koa, *Acacia Koa,* Gray

Koa, Island mahogany
(Acacia koa, Gray)
In early times the wood of the koa was extensively used by the Hawaiians for war canoes, surf boards, and calabashes. At present the wood, which has an attractive red colors and takes a high polish, is used for furniture, ukuleles, novelties and other woodwork. The tree has a beautiful round-ed canopy and may be readily distin-guished in the forests. Under favorable conditions the tree trunks attain a height of thirty or forty feet without branches, and the trees may reach seventy or more feet in height. The best koa forests are located on the Island of Hawaii.

Sisal

Indian Banyan
(Ficus Benghalensis, Linnaeus)
One of the most easily recognized trees in tropic and semi-tropic regions is the Indian banyan. Its outstanding feature is the aerial roots which grown down from more or less horizontal branches, and by supporting them enable the tree to cover a large area. Dr. Hillebrand, famous botanist and court physician, brought the first banyan to Hono-lulu from India, where it furnishes an inferior rubber, food for elephants and cattle, and fuel and shelter for humans.

Alligator or avocado pear, *Persea americana,* Miller

Alligator pear, avocado pear
(Persea americana, Miller)
The rough skin of some of the varieties of alli-gator pear has probably suggested the name. The rich, oily pulp is a favored mater-ial for the salad maker and the oil which may be extracted is used in the manufac-ture of soap and cosmetics. The color of the fruit varies from green to purple and the pulp is greenish yellow. The home of the tree is Central America.

Indian banyan, *Ficus banghalensis,* **Linnaeus**

Ohia lehua, *Metrosideros polymorpha,* **Guadichaud**

Tree fern
(Cibitum chamissoi, Kaulfuss)
The tree fern occurs in association with ohia lehua in both the dry land and moist region Hawaiian forests. It is common in the mountains of Oahu, Kauai and Maui, but may be seen at its best in Puna and near the Volcano House on the island of Hawaii. There are hundreds of thousands of acres of tree ferns on this island and some of the trunks with the fronds reach a length of more than twenty-five feet. The trunks contain an edible starch, and the young stems were used by the Hawaiians for food.

Ohia lehua
(Metrosideros polymorpha, Gaudichaud)
One of the commonest trees of the Hawaiian forest is the lehua. It grows from sea level to nearly the timber line on the mountain slopes in association with other trees and shrubs. The flowers form in bright red, terminal clusters, contain honey which attracts the native birds, and present one of the loveliest sights of the Hawaiian forests. The wood, which is hard, is sawed into timber for making flooring, furniture, and railway ties.

Kukui, candlenut tree
(Aleurites moluccana, Linnaeus)
The candle-nut was a tree of considerable usefulness to the early Hawaiians. The white kernels of the nuts were strung on the coconut leaflet midrib and burned for light; the shells, when suitably treated, yielded a black dye, and the oil when extracted, furnished a varnish for surf boards, and a waterproof coating for tapa. Unsuccessful attempts have been made to make commercial use of the oil which is of excellent quality. The candlenut tree is found on most of the Pacific islands, Java, India, and Southern China.

Tree ferns, *Cibitium chamissoi,* **Kaulfuss**

Kukui or candlenut tree, *Aleerites moluccana,* **Linnaeus**

Coconut, *Cocos nucifera*, Linnaeus

Coconut flowers, *Cocos nucifera*, Linnaeus

Coconut, *Cocos nucifera*, Linnaeus

Copra plantation, Kauai, 1912

Coconut palm
(Cocos nucifera, Linnaeus)
Probably the most familiar member of palm group is the coco palm. In areas of greater moisture and higher temperature the coco palm grows more luxuriantly than it does in Hawaii. It was very likely introduced by the early Hawaiians and much used by them. The leaves were useful for baskets and thatching and the nuts furnished both drink and food. The fibrous material from the husks of the nuts was woven into cordage and ropes, and the shells of the nuts were made into ornaments, spoons and drinking vessels. The slender, graceful trunks sometimes reach a hundred feet in height and, silhouetted against the evening sky, form the subject of many exquisite pictures.

Royal palm
(Oreodoxa Regia, Von Humboldt)
The first royal palm was planted in Honolulu by Dr. G.P. Judd, in 1850. The smooth whitened shaft is characterized by inconspicuous leaf scars, and terminates in a heavy cluster of green plumes. Some of them reach a height of a hundred feet or more.

Bird of Paradise
(Strelitzia reginae, Banks)
This novel and unusual appearing flower, a member of the banana family, is not common in Honolulu. The flowering stem springs directly from the base of the plant and rises higher than the leaves. The sheath, some six or seven inches long, is divided into six parts which spread horizontally as the flower opens. The home of the bird-of-paradise is South Africa.

Royal palms at the Schaeffer-Wodehouse home, *Oredoxa regia*, Von Humbolt

Travelers Palm, *Strelitzia reginae*, Banks

Bird of paradise, *Strelitzia reginae*, Banks

Royal palms at the Schaeffer-Wodehouse home, *Oredox regia* Von Humbolt

Palmetto palm

Screw pine, *Freycinetia arborea*, Gaudichaud

Traveller's palm
(Ravenala madagascariensis, J.F. Gmelin)
The traveler's palm is really not a palm, but a member of the banana family. Its name is derived from the fact that rain water collects in the concave bases of the leaf petioles and from which travelers may satisfy their thirst. The ironical fact is that the plant does not grow in arid regions. Its home is Madagascar.

Ieie, Climbing screw pine
(Freycinetia arborea, Gaudichaud)
This virile climber is common in the lower Hawaiian forests often forming impenetrable tangles over the ground and sending its woody stems well up to the tops of the trees. In the flowering season the deep orange to scarlet inflorescence develops and attracts the attention of even the unobservant.

Royal poinciana or flame tree, *Delonix regia,* Bojar

Royal poinciana or flame tree, *Delonix regia,* Bojar

Ilima, *Sida fallax,* Walpers

Night blooming cereus, *Hylocereus undatus,* Britten and Rosa

Night blooming cereus, *Hylocereus undatus,* Britten and Rosa

Royal poinciana, flame tree
(Delonix regia, Bojer)
Persons viewing in the off season the royal poinciana trees which line certain Honolulu streets are inclined to question their value as ornamentals. But when covered with blossoms they are the showiest and most attractive of all the flowering trees. The flowering season lasts more than half the year. The trees are at their best in June and July. The seed pods which hang on the trees most of the year are flat, thick, of moderate length, somewhat curved and filled with dark, elongated seeds frequently used in leis.

Ilima
(Sida fallax, Walpers)
There are a number of species of ilima in the Hawaiian Islands and it was formerly a common practice to make leis from the flowers. Orange-colored crepe paper has now been largely substituted for the ilima flowers in lei making. It is the emblematic flower for the island of Oahu. The ilima grows at lower elevations and blooms most of the year.

False wiliwili, Red sandalwood
(Adenanthera pavonina, Linnaeus)
The false wiliwili is a slender, rapid-growing tree, seldom reaching more than twenty-five feet in height, best known for its shining bright red lens-shaped seeds, extensively used in making seed beads or leis.

Red ginger, *Fiji nutanus*, Roscoe

White ginger, *Hedychium gardnerianum*, Roscoe

Shell ginger, *Alpinia nutanus*, Roscoe .

White ginger
(Hedychium gardnerianum, Roscoe)
There are more than half a dozen species of ginger found in Hawaii, some wild, others cultivated. They are all distinguished by their delicate, attractive and sweet-scented flowers. Most of them have been introduced from the Far East.

Ape
(Alocasia macrorrhiza, Schott)
This conspicuous garden plant, which is a native of southern Asia, has been introduced in many Pacific islands. The large, heart-shaped, highly ornate leaves rise from heavy stems to the height of an ordinary man. In times of scarcity portions of a native ape were used for food by the early Hawaiians. The flowers of the ape are packed on a long spike which is enclosed in a pinkish yellow sheath.

Kiawe or algaroba, *Prosopis juliflora*, Schwartz

Ape, *Alocasia macrorrhiza*, Schott

Algaroba, Kiawe, mesquite
(Prosopis juliflora, Schwartz)
One of the most useful trees in Hawaii is the algaroba or mesquite. The wood of the trunk furnishes fuel, the flowers an excellent honey and the waxy seed pods fodder for hogs and cattle. Moreover, it thrives on sandy shores and arid plains where few other trees will grow. In 1828 the first tree was planted in Hawaii by Father Bachelot.

False wiliwili or red sandalwood, *Adenanthera pavonina*, Linnaeus

Hibiscus, *Hibiscus tiliaceus*, **Linnaeus**

Hau, *Hibiscus tiliaceus*, **Linnaeus**

Hibiscus, *Hibiscus tiliaceus*, **Linnaeus**

Hibiscus
(Hibiscus tiliaceus, Linnaeus)
Fresh flowers come each day throughout the year, but they last only a single day. Many lovely forms and color patterns have been produced by crossing these common varieties with introduced plants.

Hau
(Hibiscus tiliaceus, Linnaeus)
When growing in the natural state the hau becomes an almost impenetrable network of stems and branches. In gardens it may be trained over trellises and arbors where it forms a delightful canopy. The flowers, which are borne abundantly, open bright yellow in color, but change at the end of the day or the following morning to dull orange or salmon color, to deep red.

Bougainvillea, *Bougainvillea spectabilis*, **Willdenow**

Bombax, *Bombax ellipticum*, **Von Humbolt**

Airplant flowers, *Bryophyllum pinnatum*

Bougainvillea
(Bougainvillea spectabilis, Wildenow)
The bougainvillea is a strong woody vine which trails over fences, walls, buildings and trellises. Its stiff, sharp thorns give it firm, secure hold on its support. The flowers, which are small, yellowish and tubular, are surrounded by a cup consisting of three bright-colored bracts. There are several varieties and the color of the bracts varies from purple to rose red. Flowers are borne most of the year.

Bombax
(Bombax ellipticum, Van Humboldt)
Most of the year this sparsely branched tree seems to offer little to justify planting it as an ornamental but during the winter months slender buds, with explosive suddenness, open into handsome flowers. The buds are purplish outside, downy white within, and when open expose many long, pink or white stamens.

Hawaiian poppy, *Puakala*

Nuuanu Pali with a protective wooden fence on the left and a new concrete wall on the right, 1912

11" x 14" VIEWS

Ray Jerome Baker made photography look easy. He was an acute observer, a master craftsman and a tireless experimenter. Outgoing and friendly in personality, he inspired great trust in his subjects. Today's viewers have no trouble entering the world he captured on film.

Baker enjoyed talking about the subjects of his photographs but he disliked being asked "how" he took them. He preferred not to discuss his methods unless he was actually teaching students·in a classroom.

"Personally," Baker once wrote, "I do not feel competent to tell people who seek advice about their cameras and the exposures. There are so many cameras, some with fancy assets, that I know little about and I do not handle these cameras."

The photographs in this section of *Hawaiian Yesterdays* were taken by Baker with large-format 11"x 14" cameras. He had several during his lifetime, beginning with a second-hand model that he purchased from a real estate salesman in Eureka.

"I had never used anything making negatives that large," Baker wrote in *Odyssey of a Cameraman*" (1964), "but since he offered the equipment at a low price I decided to buy it. He pointed out that his rapid rectilinear lens was a very fine one, made by one of the very old lens makers.

"The lens was relatively slow by later standards and it had no shutter. Exposures were made with the lens cap, a method which proved quite successful because there were seldom moving objects in the landscapes photographed and the large groups were cautioned to keep still.

"I began using the camera and made some very fine negatives of California's giant redwoods. Later the camera became damaged and I purchased a new one, but the lens I still have after fifty years."

One of the cameras that Baker gave to the Bishop Museum was an 11 x 14 box camera that he made himself out of heavy cardboard. He mounted an old lens on the front and loaded the camera in his darkroom. After taking a picture he returned to the darkoom, unloaded the single sheet of exposed film and put in a new one.

"Attractive scenes in the larger sizes sold readily," Baker explained in his description of the camera for the museum, "and because it was more economical, both in time and material to make contact prints instead of enlargements, I chose to make large negatives. This cardboard box was made in an afternoon and many fine negatives were made with it."

It was "one shot camera" because it had to be loaded in the darkroom. Perhaps this was all to the good, because it meant the very careful selection of the subject and exceptional care in setting up and making the exposure."

Moana Hotel, from the corner of what was the entrance to the Cleghorn Estate, Ainahau, 1912

Kapiolani Park. Makee Island. In the distance is the present Kapahulu Avenue, then called Makee Road, 1912

Entrance to Ainahau from Kalakaua Avenue, 1910. This is the present Kaiulani Avenue. To the left is the Princess Kaiulani Hotel and on the right is the Hemmeter Center.

Diamond Head from the front of the
"House Without A Key," Halekulani
Hotel, 1915

The entrance to the Damon Estate,
Moanalua Gardens, 1910

189—

The Royal Hawaiian Hotel, later the
Armed Forces YMCA, 1912

Pigeon loft and a muscovy duck pond, now the site of the American Savings and Loan (Pan Am) Building on Kapiolani Boulevard, 1910

Mullet pond and banana trees, Kalakaua Avenue, 1912. On the left in later
years was the Wagon Wheel Restaurant.
Now Olohana Street, this site is occupied
by the Gateway Hotel and Nick's
Fishmarket

Ward Estate and the Old Plantation,
1912

193—

The famous monkey pod tree at the
Damon Estate, Moanalua, 1910

— 194

Ward Estate and the Old Plantation
(today a parking lot, 1912

Date palms at entrance to Queens Hospital, 1910

Grass house in Kapiolani Park, near Makee Island and the present Kapahulu Avenue, 1910

The town of Wailuku, Maui, 1912

Coconut Island in Kaneohe Bay, looking back toward the Koolau Range, 1912

Grass shack, near Kilauea, Kauai, 1910

Grass shack, near Kilauea, Kauai, 1912

201

Waimea Canyon, Kauai, 1912

Kekaha Plantation Mill, Kekaha, Kauai,
1914

Hanalei Valley, Kauai, 1912

Beach at Hanalei, Kauai, 1910

207-4

The Rice family hotel, Lihue, Kauai, 1916

Along the Kohala Ditch Trail, a self portrait of R.J. Baker, 1912

In 1933 Baker was hired by Inter-Island Airways
to take photographs for its initial advertising
campaign. Aside from meeting his obligations
to the company, he took this opportunity to
make the first civilian aerial documentary
of the Hawaiian Islands.

Flying over Punchbowl, 1950

ABOVE HAWAII

Hawaii's first airplane flight took place on Dec. 31, 1910. On that afternoon over 3,000 Islanders paid $1 apiece to watch a mainland pilot, James C. "Bud" Mars, as he took off from the Moanalua Polo Field in his flimsy Curtis "Skylark" and circled the area at 500 feet. Five minutes later the plane landed amidst wild applause.

Mars made three other flights that afternoon and then returned to Honolulu for an evening of celebration. "I find your Hawaiian air currents rather rough ones," he said later, "but everything else was lovely."

Ray Jerome Baker was among the spectators at Moanalua. He took several photos of the plane in flight and others of Mars standing in front of the aircraft. It was a historic day that awakened Baker's lifetime interest in aviation.

Nine years later, on March 26, 1919, Major Hugh Kneer, an Army aviator from Ford Island in Pearl Harbor, completed the first inter-Island flight. It took him three hours and nine minutes to fly from Honolulu to Hilo.

The first successful California-Hawaii flight was made in 1927 by Army lieutenants Lester Maitland and A. F. Hegenberger. From Oakland it took the pair 25 hours, 49 minutes and 30 seconds to reach Wheeler Field in their tri-motored Fokker monoplane. Only a month earlier Charles A. Lindbergh had received a hero's welcome in Paris after he landed the *Spirit of St. Louis* following a non-stop flight from New York.

Inter-Island Airways pioneered passenger service in 1929 between Honolulu and Hilo with two eight-passenger Sikorsky and Amphibian S-38s. The S-38s were able to operate from either land or water, climbed well and had a top speed of 125 mph. Flight time between the islands was three hours.

Although airplanes were fast and economical it took several years for Inter-Island to convince people that they were also trouble-free. Safety was a primary concern of company president Stanley C. Kennedy, an ex-World War I pilot from Honolulu who had also become interested in aviation after the "Bud" Mars flight in 1910. "We had to give people the feel of flying first," Kennedy once explained, "so they could see it was safe as well as fun; give them an aerial view of the Island, and just generally get them used to flying in a plane."

In 1933, Baker was hired by Inter-Island Airways to help educate hesitant passengers by taking aerial photographs from their aircraft. Some of his pictures, taken with a large 8 x 10 camera, were pure landscape views designed to lure potential travellers into the air to see for themselves. Others were more promotional and included the company's second plane as it flew above Oahu and the Neighbor Islands.

Honolulu Harbor and downtown. The long street running
vertically is Nuuanu Avenue, 1933

Honolulu and Aloha Tower, 1933

Flying over Manoa Valley toward St. Louis Heights, 1933

Flying over St. Louis Heights, towards Palolo Valley. Top street in St. Louis Heights is the corner of Maigret and Alencastre, 1933

Plane flying toward Koko Crater, 1933. The valley to the left behind the crater is now Hawaii Kai and is occupied by thousands of homes.

Inter-Island Airways plane flying toward Koko Head Crater. At the bottom is Hanauma Bay and on the left is Lunalilo Home. This was the former Marconi Wireless Station, 1933

Airplane flying over Makapuu Point. To the left is
Waimanalo and on the right is Rabbit Island, 1933

Looking through Nuuanu Pali gap toward Honolulu, 1933

Coastline near Mokuleia, Oahu and Kaena Point to the right, 1933

218

North shore of Oahu coastline, 1933

The town of Waianae, the plantation and the mill, 1933

Schofield Barracks, Oahu, 1933

Tripler Hospital, 1950

Town of Kalaupapa, 1933

Kahului Harbor, Kahului, Maui, 1933

Town of Wailuku, Maui, looking up into Iao Valley, 1933

Town and sugar plantations to the rear of Lahaina, Maui, 1933

Interior of Haleakala crater, Maui, 1933

The point, pier, church, sugar mill and tiny village of Hana, Maui, 1933

Laupahoehoe, Hawaii, 1933. The village and school were destroyed in a 1946 tidal wave.

Niulii Plantation, Kohala, Hawaii, 1933

Papaaloa Mill and Village, 1933

Pepeekeo Mill, village and plantation, Hawaii, 1933

Hakalau Plantation, mill and village, Hawaii, 1933

Paahau plantation and mill, Hawaii, 1933

Haina Landing below Honokaa, Hawaii with its molasses bins at the bottom, 1933

Waipio Valley, Hawaii, 1933

Steam and smoke clouds, Mokuaweoweo, Hawaii, looking southwest, 1933

231

Nawiliwili Harbor, Kauai, 1933

Mountains and coast looking toward Port Allen, 1933

Port Allen, formerly the main harbor on Kauai, 1933

"Aloha" title slide that Baker used to end his public presentations

Early Photographers in Hawaii

Ray Jerome Baker was the first-known photo historian in the Hawaiian Islands. In addition to taking his own pictures he collected the work of others and did research on the photographers who were here before him. It is due to his pioneering efforts and foresight that so much of Hawaii's past has been saved for future generations.

Baker tried to track down as much information as he could on the early photographers in Hawaii. In the 1930's and 1940's he read old newspapers, interviewed surviving family members and sought out forgotten albums in second-hand bookstores. He was interested in all aspects of Hawaiian history but photography, in particular, fascinated him.

Jacques Arago, an artist who accompanied the Louis de Freycinet expedition to Hawaii in 1819, apparently brought a portable reflex camera obscura along with him on the corvette *Uranie*. He used it as an aid in sketching people and landscapes.

This rectangular box, an ancestor of the modern reflex camera, had a glass lens in front and a mirror inside which directed the image formed to a frosted glass plate on which the artist placed translucent paper. Arago mentions the camera obscura in his account of the trip, *Narrative of a Voyage round the World*, published in London in 1823.

In 1845, Theophilus Metcalf took out an advertisement in *The Polynesian* announcing that he was available to take daguerreotype portraits between 9 a.m. and 1 p.m. each day in his rooms above the newspaper's office. His price was $10 for each picture plus $2 for a miniature case to display it in. No earlier mention of a daguerreotypist in Hawaii has been found.

The daguerreotype was the earliest photographic process to achieve popular success. Invented by Louis Jacques Daguerre and announced in 1839, this method produced a direct positive image on a sensitized metal plate. After a few minutes of exposure in the camera the plate's image was developed and fixed. Because this process produced no negatives, every daguerreotype was a unique, one-of-a-kind photograph.

Metcalf, a civil engineer who primarily took photographs as a hobby, lived in Hawaii from 1842 until his death in 1866. Unfortunately none of his daguerreotypes, if they still exist, have been identified.

On February 3, 1847 the front page of *The Sandwich Island News* stated that "Daguerreotype mania" had come to Honolulu. The paper went on to report that a photographer that called himself Senor Le Bleu was doing a brisk business taking portraits for $6 apiece. Le Bleu already had "engagements for weeks in advance."

But Senor Le Bleu, like Metcalf, vanished without leaving records or known work behind. It was not until 1853 when Stephen Goodfellow and Hugo Stangenwald arrived in Honolulu that photographers began to leave their mark in Hawaii.

Together the two men opened the Daguerran Gallery at the corner of Merchant and Fort streets. When Goodfellow left shortly thereafter, Stangenwald continued alone and moved his studio to the corner of Fort and King.

Stangenwald established a lucrative portrait business in Honolulu. Many members of the royal family were among his clients. He also left behind the first scenic views of the Islands.

In 1856 Stangenwald visited San Francisco and then returned to Hawaii and introduced both ambrotypes (glass negatives backed by black paint or paper) and paper prints made from the wet collodion process. For the later method a glass plate was coated in the dark with collodion (a mixture of alcohol, ether and gun cotton), dipped in silver nitrate, and exposed when wet. Multiple prints could be made by contact printing the paper against the negative.

Wet plates were gradually replaced by the dry plate process. The plates were coated with a gelatin emulsion which dried before the exposure was made.

But in 1858, Stangenwald stopped his professional photography and went to the mainland to continue his earlier studies in medicine. By the time he returned as a doctor in 1860 the photography business in Hawaii was booming.

In late 1861, newspaper advertisements announced that photographer Joseph W. King had set up his photography business above the offices of the *Pacific Commercial Advertiser* next door to the Post Office. The studio had previously been operated by W. F. Howland and King may have worked as Howland's assistant before taking over the space.

By August, 1862, King was advertising in *The Friend,* that he had "entirely refitted and renovated the rooms occupied by H. Stangenwald (more recently by E. D. Durant) and hopes by strict attention to the tastes and fancies of his customers to receive a share of the public patronage." There are no definite dates on King's arrival in Hawaii—the date 1858 appears on the back of several existing photographs—but his last public appearance was better noted.

Readers of the *Pacific Commercial Advertiser* learned on August 6, 1870 that King's studio had been raided by the town marshall who had found "indecent and obscene pictures." King was summoned before the police magistrate and pleaded guilty to the charge of "maintaining a public nuisance." A week later the newspaper reported that King had been fined $100 for his traffic in obscenity."

No further mention of King was made by the newspaper and the records of his hearing before the magistrate have disappeared. Gone, too, are the "obscene" photographs seized as evidence in the raid on King's studio. On December 31, a Chinese photographer, Yat Sing, announced in the *Pacific Commercial Advertiser* that he had "fitted up rooms lately occupied by J. W. King" above the newspaper offices.

Another important photographer of the period is Charles L. Weed, a California landscape photographer who came to Honolulu from San Francisco in March, 1865. He remained here only until November, 1865 when he continued on to Hong Kong. During his brief residence, Weed was quite active in taking pictures and making large albumen prints.

He took numerous studio portraits with his large glass plate camera and shot spectacular views of Honolulu from Punchbowl, Nuuanu Pali and Haleakala Crater on Maui. He was the first photographer in Hawaii to take panoramic sequences.

Henry L. Chase opened his Honolulu studio in 1862, renting the same rooms formerly occupied by Howland and then King. Four years later he moved to a new Fort and Hotel Street location and in 1870 to yet another studio across Fort Street above the store of Grunwald &

Schutte.

Chase kept his original negatives instead of selling them to his customers along with their prints. He thus put together an extensive collection of negatives recording the sights and people of Hawaii.

He left Honolulu in 1874 to live in New Hampshire but returned with his cameras two years later. Unfortunately, Chase's studio was destroyed in a fire on March 18, 1877. The blaze wiped out his valuable negative collection as well as his equipment and supplies.

Although Chase did not give up photography after the fire, his business never regained its foothold in Honolulu. He began to spend most of his time taking photographs on the Neighbor Islands. In 1886 he moved to Wailuku, Maui, where he died penniless in 1901.

Born in Denmark, Christian J. Hedemann arrived at Maui in 1878 to work as a sugar mill engineer in Hana. He taught himself photography before moving to Oahu in 1884 and taking a job at the Honolulu Iron Works.

Kodak began selling its amateur cameras locally in 1889 and that same year Hedemann helped start, as president, the Hawaiian Camera Club. It had a membership of about 50 amateur photographers. The group presented several amateur photography shows in Honolulu but lasted only until 1893, the year Queen Liliuokalani was overthrown to end the monarchy.

In 1895 the Pocket Kodak Camera began to be mass produced and in 1898 the Folding Pocket Kodak Camera, forerunner of the modern roll-film camera, was introduced. The popular Brownie Camera was launched in 1900. Suddenly, everyone started to take pictures.

When Ray Jerome Baker first visited Hawaii in 1908, he met the photographer James J. Williams. Williams had arrived himself in 1879 as an unskilled laborer and soon found employment with photographer Menzies Dickson who had opened his studio in 1867.

Dickson sent Williams to the U.S. East Coast to study photography. Alex, Williams' grandson, stated in a 1979 *Honolulu* magazine interview that during this trip Williams met Matthew Brady, famed for his company's coverage of the Civil War. It was Brady's practice to pose his portraits in order to make them appear more natural.

Back in Honolulu, Dickson was apparently tiring of the photography business. He sold his studio to Williams in 1880 and left to manage the Kawailoa Cattle Ranch at Waialua. Williams did a good business in portraiture and landscape pictures. He also sold through local shops on commission. Williams founded *Paradise of the Pacific* (the ancestor of today's *Honolulu* magazine) in 1888 and presented the first issue to King Kalakaua.

Baker sometimes used Williams' studio on Fort Street after becoming a permanent resident in 1910 for developing and printing. In return he taught Williams the latest photographic developments and furnished him with landscape pictures that he could sell.

Williams grew deaf in his later years and in 1926, at the age of 72, he was struck near his studio by the running board of a street car. He was taken to Queen's Hospital where he died of a skull fracture and internal injuries. His son, James A. Williams, subsequently took over the business.

Another of Baker's good friends was Norman D. Hill, a photographer who operated from his studio-home on Akoko Lane and specialized in copying and retouching historic photographs. He sometimes took Baker's original landscape negatives and "improved" them by turning ordinary daytime shots into moonlight scenes, complete with a shimmer of light across the water.

Hill died in 1937, at age 56, of an overdose of sleeping pills. His will left his books to the library, his art collection to the Honolulu Academy of Arts and his photographic equipment to Baker. It took two car trips to Hill's studio for Baker to load up everything and take it home.

During the 1920's and 1930's, Baker grew into his prime as an artist. The death of Williams had made him aware of his own mortality and he became more determined than ever to leave behind a significant body of photography for the people of Hawaii.

NOTE: Readers who want to learn more about Hawaii's early photographers are urged to visit the Bernice P. Bishop Museum. Staff members and volunteer workers in the Ray Jerome Baker Room are actively engaged in researching the Pacific's photographic history.

In 1980, the centennial year of Baker's birth, the museum sponsored an exhibit entitled *Na Pa'i Ki'i: The Photographers in the Hawaiian Islands, 1845-1900*. The display was coordinated by Lynn Davis, curator of photography. Ms. Davis also authored an attractive catalog of the exhibition which is published by the Bishop Museum Press.

Another valuable sourcebook is *Photographers of Old Hawaii*, written by Joan Abramson and published by Island Heritage. It includes a general survey of local photography, biographical sketches and numerous photographs.

Chronology

1880	Ray Jerome Baker born December 1, at Owen Center, near Rockford, Illinois.
1881	Family moved to Brownsdale Village, near Austin, Minnesota.
1898-1902	Attended the Mechanic Arts High School in St. Paul, Minnesota.
1903	Became a professional photographer after attending the University of Minnesota for one semester.
1904-1910	Operated a photo studio in Eureka, California.
1906	Married Edith Mary Frost in Eureka, California on Nov. 21.
1908	First visited Hawaii from February to June.
1909	Earl Frost Baker, their only child, is born.
1910	Learned how to take motion pictures from Thomas Edison. Returned to live in Honolulu.
1911	Rented a cottage at 1679 Beach Road.
1912	Photographed extensively on Lanai.
1913	Operated a photo studio with E. L. Edgeworth.
1914	Began making colored lantern slides. Had his first major slide showing in Honolulu at the Opera House.
1915	Bought a house and property at 1911 Kalakaua Avenue.
1917	Toured Japan and Korea.
1918	Took motion pictures of Kilauea erupting on the Big Island. Lectured about his trip to Japan before the California Camera Club in San Francisco.
1919-1920	Lectured on *Hawaii, The Land of Heart's Desire* for the Midland Chautauqua Circuit.
1922	Took a trip to Palmyra Island.
1925	Toured Australia and New Zealand as a cameraman for Pathe News.
1926	Became interested in time-lapse photography.
1927	Presented weekly motion picture programs about Hawaii for tourists at the Moana Hotel.
1928	Lectured at the University of Hawaii on the subject of Motion Pictures as an aid to Scientific Research.
1931	Took motion pictures of the U.S.S. Chicago's South Pacific "shakedown" cruise.
1933	Lectured for the Extension Division of the University of Hawaii and at the Library of Hawaii. Hired by

Inter-Island Airways to take aerial views of the Hawaiian Islands.

1934 Granted a Bachelor of Science degree from the University of Hawaii. Lectured at Field Museum in Chicago on the subject of *Hawaiian Volcanoes*.

1936 Photographed the Oahu Sugar Company's plantation and factory for the University of the State of New York. Published a limited edition of *The Romance of Raw Sugar*.

1937 Taught photography at the YMCA.

1938 Edith Baker suffered a paralytic stroke from which she never recovered. Between 1940 and her death in 1952 she was nursed by a sister in California.

1939 Published a limited edition of his original *Hawaiian Yesterdays*.

1941-1946 Worked exclusively as a portrait photographer during World War II.

1948 Expelled from the Honolulu Lions Club for bringing Dr. John E. Reinecke, a suspected Communist, to a club luncheon. The club reinstated him after threatened legal action but he resigned immediately afterwards.

1949 Toured Mexico. Produced the film *Mexican Pilgrimage*.

1953 Toured Central America

1950 Donated his three motion pictures to the George Eastman Museum in Rochester, N.Y. They were later given to the Bishop Museum.

1951 Toured the West Indies.

1952 Toured Alaska. Produced the film *Alaska Journey*.

1954 Visited 25 countries in Asia and Europe. Exhibited photographs from the trip in the lobby of the Library of Hawaii.

1955 Toured South America.

1956 Toured Europe. Gave 5,000 catalogued negatives to the Bishop Museum.

1957 Toured New Zealand.

1958 Toured the Soviet Union.

1960 Made his last significant photographs, on the Neighbor Islands, in the company of Robert E. Van Dyke. Bequeathed his property and a collection of photographs and equipment to the Bishop Museum.

1964 Published a limited edition of his autobiography, *Odyssey of a Cameraman*.

1972 Died October 27, in Honolulu, at age 91.

BIBLIOGRAPHY

BOOKS

1912

Beginning in 1912, Ray Jerome Baker began making up souvenir albums of original photographs for his customers. These were usually 5 x 7 inches in size, bound in leather and given such titles as *Alohaland, Hawaii,* or *Hawaii-Nei.* They contained anywhere from 25 to 100 photographs each and substitutions were often made as the years progressed. Baker kept the most popular albums in stock at his studio and printed others by special order in about five days. He produced several hundred of these from 1912 to 1935.

1914
Hawaiian Types
Palms and other Flora of the Hawaiian Islands
Hawaiian Island Views
Homes, Historical Buildings and Places of Interest in the Hawaiian Islands

This series of four booklets was published in 1914 by *Paradise of the Pacific* magazine. Each was priced at 75 cents a copy. Baker had a half-interest in these booklets, all of which contained his photographs as well as others by R. W. Perkins, R. K. Bonine and J. J. Williams. There were 2,500 copies of each booklet printed and they were available until 1916.

1936
The Romance of Raw Sugar
"A collection of photographs whose purpose is to show the processes of growing sugar cane and producing raw sugar in Hawaii. Prepared in most part on the plantation of Oahu Sugar Company in the months of May and June, 1936, for the University of the State of New York." Photographs by Ray Jerome Baker. Text by William Wolters, agriculturist, Oahu Sugar Company. Between 85 and 100 photographs.

The popularity of *The Romance of Raw Sugar* convinced Baker that there was a market for limited-edition books of original photographs. During the next quarter-century he produced over two dozen of these in his Kalakaua Avenue studio. He printed and bound them himself, in a variety of bindings, and gold-stamped the title on the cover. It is difficult to say how many copies of each title were actually published because he likely only assembled enough to meet the demand. The number of photos in each book may vary from copy to copy. As each book was finished he would often send inspection copies to libraries, businesses and individuals on his mailing list whom he thought might be interested in purchasing it. They would either send back the book or a check by return mail. Prices ranged from $5 to $50 per copy depending on his costs.

1938
Familiar Hawaiian Flowers
"A collection of original photographs of native and ornamental fruits, flowers, trees and shrubs growing in Hawaii." Photographs and text by Ray Jerome Baker. Hand coloring by Edith M. Baker.

Baker issued this book in two different versions. There was a large edition, with 133 subjects listed in the index but actually containing up to 150 prints. It was priced at $50. The smaller edition included 54 prints and sold for $25. *Familiar Hawaiian Flowers* proved to be a very popular title and copies were issued for several years. After his wife suffered a stroke in 1938, Baker hired Martha Barton to do some of his hand coloring.

1938
Camera Studies in Portraiture
"A series of original photographs of people made over a period of years and assembled and published in 1938." Photographs by Ray Jerome Baker. It contained from 50 to 100 photographs dating from his arrival in 1908.

1938
Hawaii: The Isle of a Thousand Wonders
"A comprehensive collection of original photographs of points of interest on Hawaii, the largest island of the Hawaiian group, taken in the month of April, 1938. A few pictures of earlier date are included." This title went through several editions in several sizes and with varying amounts of photographs. A 1948 edition is in the collection of Robert E. Van Dyke.

1938
Alohaland
"A collection of original photographs that reflect the atmosphere and spirit of Hawaii Nei. Photographed and arranged by Ray Jerome Baker, together with the famous prose poem by Mark Twain and an interpretation in verse by Will Sabin." There were 51 photographs in this book with each plate preceded by a guard sheet with printed description. All of the prints were made from 11 by 14 inch negatives and trimmed down to book size.

1938
Early Hawaiian Prints
"Photographed and assembled by Ray Jerome Baker. A collection of photographic reproductions of Hawaiian prints which were printed from copper plates engraved in the early years of the nineteenth century." The plates were copied directly from the original paintings and sketches made on location by contemporary artists and explorers." Each of the 102 prints were preceded by a guard sheet with printed description.

1939
Hawaiian Yesterdays
"A tale in pictures of Hawaiian life in the days that are gone. By Ray Jerome Baker. A collection of original camera studies, made on various island of the Hawaiian Group, of the intimate life and activities of Hawaiian people between the years 1908 - 1920." It contained 50 prints.

1941
Honolulu Then and Now
"A photographic record of progress in the City of Honolulu." Each of the 172 prints is preceded by a guard sheet and printed with description. Most of the photographs were taken by Baker from 1908 to 1940 but others, dating back to the 1850's are included for contrast. The initial binding was a light-blue linen-like cloth with a paper label on the cover and spine. This was not found to be suitable and later copies were bound with a dark-blue patterned cloth with the title stamped in gold on the cover and spine.

1943
Scenic Hawaii
"A collection of unusual photographs of the Hawaiian Islands by Ray Jerome Baker." Tongg Publishing Company editions of 1943, 1944, and 1945. This is one of the few Baker volumes printed outside his studio by a commercial publisher. It contains 64 pages and is made up of substantially the same photographs as Alohaland along with an identical text. About 100,000 copies were printed.

1945
Men of our Armed Forces
"A study in faces of our fighting men. A collection of original portraits of men of the armed forces of the United States of America, taken in Honolulu during the years 1942-1945." This was a small edition containing 152 original portraits and eight pages of text. Baker printed them mainly for his friends and a few institutions.

1945
Art Forms in Plant Structures
"A series of original photographs of plant material from nature's own art gallery." Contained 97 prints. Several copies were made up with hand colored plates.

1946
Sanford B. Dole, 1844 -1926
"A group of photographs made from unretouched negatives taken on Mr. Dole's 80th birthday, April 23, 1924." There were 26 portraits in the Dole series but when Baker looked through his files to produce this book he found many of them ruined through physical deterioration. He included 10 prints in the published book.

1946
A Brief History of the Lions Club of Honolulu 1926-1946
Authorized by the Board of Directors and prepared by the History Committee, 1946. Committee chairman and editor, Ray Jerome Baker." Although this book represents a publication of the Lions Club it was written and completely paid for by Baker. It contained 102 pages, including frontispiece and illustrations, and was printed by the Hawaiian Printing Company.

1948
Scenic Hawaii
"A series of photographs taken on all the islands in the Hawaiian Group." This was basically a souvenir album of original Baker photographs. It went through many editions (some earlier than the above date) in several sizes over the years. The amount of photographs may vary per copy.

1948
Some Descendants of Tryal Baker, 1685-1776
"A narrative of a Pioneer family by Ray Jerome Baker. Illustrated with photographic reproductions of recent as well as earlier family portraits." This book was not intended to be sold but was instead produced for Baker's brothers and sisters and their families. It included 61 pages of text, two blank pages for notes and 43 photographs.

1950
Sketches and Maps of Old Honolulu
"Including the Choris sketch of Honolulu Fort, 1818, the Dana sketch of Honolulu, 1840, and the Clint view of the harbor, about 1872; together with numerous general and detailed maps of the city." This book contains 32 plates, each preceded by a guard sheet with printed description. A second printing was made in 1952.

1950
Honolulu in 1853
"Six photographic reproductions of the lithographs made from original drawings by Paul Emmert in 1853, together with brief descriptions of occupants, owners and locations of the subjects drawn." Baker made the reproductions and wrote a text for this slim book which contained six plates.

1951
Honolulu in 1870
"A series of ten rare and hitherto unpublished photographs, taken of the city in the autumn of 1870, from the Union Street Bell Tower, by Henry L. Chase, Honolulu, photographer; a brief summary of events in the period 1868-1873, concise data on business firms and personalities of the period, together with some social and economic considerations." This book contained 11 plates, each preceded by a guard sheet with descriptive text.

1951
Odyssey of a Cameraman
This autobiographical narrative went through several editions in 1951, 1952 and 1953. The amount of photographs varied from 35 to 80 and copies were presented to friends, family members and libraries. Primarily photographs with little text.

1952
Racial Studies
This was not a bound book but rather a portfolio of 55 photographs.

1954
Princess Kaiulani
"A brief biographical sketch of Hawaii's beloved Princess, together with a series of portraits showing her from childhood to adult life." This small book contained 12 photographs, each preceded by a guard sheet with descriptive text. A second edition was issued in 1955. The plates were printed for this edition by Tongg Publishing Company while Baker printed the text and did the binding.

1964
Odyssey of a Cameraman
"An epic in text and pictures which tells of experiences and travels in many lands, the life story of a man who began working when photography was still young, and who followed it professionally more than sixty years. He witnessed the early beginnings of motion pictures, the advent of sound and finally the coming of color to the screen." This revised edition of his 1951 book carries no date but was printed by Tongg Publishing Company in June, 1964. It contained 153 pages of text and 68 photographs.

ARTICLES
Baker's personal scrapbooks contain articles that he wrote for various periodicals dating back to 1906. Unfortunately, they are seldom dated or identified to the magazine or newspaper they appeared in. The following is a partial list of his contributions to Mid-Pacific Magazine and Paradise of the Pacific.

Mid-Pacific Magazine
For many years Baker was referred to as the official photographer for Mid-Pacific Magazine. His photographs appeared in almost every issue and he shot more than half of its covers.

Volume XIV No. 4 October, 1917
"With My Camera In Japan," pages 332-341.

Volume XIV No. 5 November, 1917
"My Visit to the MARU-NI, the second of a series of Illustrated Articles on the Picturesque Orient," pages 436-445.

Volume XIV No. 6 December, 1917
"The Ainu of Japan," pages 580-587.

Volume XV No. 1 January, 1918
"With My Camera in Korea," pages 82-87.

Volume XV No. 2 February, 1918
"About the Hermit Kingdom with a Camera," pages 180-183.

Volume XLVII No. 4 October-December, 1935
"Racial Patterns in Hawaii," pages 317-322.

Paradise of the Pacific
Volume 55 No. 10 October, 1943
"Honolulu A Century Ago," pages 14-16, 59.

Volume 56 No. 10 October, 1944
"The Case of the Wild Bullock," pages 24-26.

Volume 57 No. 10 October 1945
"Kamehameha Statue in Kohala," pages 23-24.

Volume 57 No. 11 November, 1945
"Kamehameha Statue in Kohala," pages 6-7, 31.

Volume 58 No. 1 January 1946
"Honolulu's First Photographer," pages 21-22.

Volume 58 No. 3 March, 1946
"Tour of Oahu Seventy-three Years Ago," pages 20-23.

Volume 62 No. 12 December, 1950
"The Oahu Charity School," pages 56-58.

Volume 63 ANNUAL EDITION, 1952
"Honolulu in 1870," pages 55-58.

Volume 64 ANNUAL EDITION, 1953
"Movie Making in Pioneer Days," pages 60-62, 122-123.

Volume 66 ANNUAL EDITION, 1954
"A visit to Palmyra Island," pages 43-47.

Volume 67 ANNUAL EDITION, 1955
"Promoting Hawaii on the Chautauqua Circuits," pages 21-23.

Volume 68 No. 11 November, 1956
"This Was Honolulu . . . less than fifty years ago," pages 38-40.

Volume 69 ANNUAL EDITION, 1956
"Norman Hill . . . photographer's poet," pages 58-59.

LETTERS
Baker bound his outgoing letters, both personal and business, from 1918 to 1966. He presented these volumes to Robert E. Van Dyke along with assorted diaries and other material. Sometime later, however, Baker borrowed back his letters for the years 1956 to 1966 and promised to return them. He never did and they have apparently disappeared.

From 1939 to 1964, Baker wrote and distributed an annual news letter at the end of each year. In the early years these were mimeographed but later they were professionally typed and reproduced by offset. The series from 1954 to 1964 was typed by Mrs. Jean Dodge from Baker's manuscript.

TRAVEL REPORTS
South American Adventure 1955
"A brief report on a flight to seven South American countries, with intimate glimpses of life and activities of Latin-American People." Several sets of this 27-page report, some containing photographs, were bound and given to close friends.

European Diary (1956)
"A brief report of a steamer voyage from Honolulu to Europe and a motor tour of eight Western European countries; together with some social and historical observations by Ray Jerome Baker." Several sets of this 30-page report were bound and given to close friends.

New Zealand Land of Enchantment (1957)
"A brief report on a re-visit to the Dominion of New Zealand. Together with some social and economic considerations, by Ray Jerome Baker." Several sets of this 20 -page report were bound and given to close friends.

Inside Russia (1958)
"A brief report on a tour of the Soviet Union visiting the great cities of Leningrad, Kiev, Odessa, Yalta, Sochi, Kharkov and Moscow." Several sets of this 20 -page report were bound and given to close friends.

MISCELLANEOUS
A Brief History
of the Hawaiian Trail and Mountain Club
"Compiled from the Official and Other Records of the Club in 1954 by R. J. Baker." This 127-page typed manuscript is now in the collection of Robert E. Van Dyke.

The Photographers of the Hawaiian Islands 1847-1957
"A brief biographical sketch on each of the professional photographers who practiced in the Hawaiian Islands from 1847-1957 along with sketches of those who were not in business but left behind such material as to be included in this study." This 366-page typed manuscript is now in the collection of Robert E. Van Dyke. Baker intended it to be published along with examples of each photographer's work.

The Artists of the Hawaiian Islands 1778-1960
"A study, with hundreds of illustrations of all of the major known artists, who have visited, lived in, worked in and passed their days in the Hawaiian Islands, from the time of the Discovery of Hawaii in 1778 by Capt. James Cook to the present. A biographical sketch of each and examples of their work." This 819-page typed manuscript (two volumes) is now in the collection of Robert E. Van Dyke.

The City of Honolulu
"A history and study of the city of Honolulu from the earliest settlements by the native Hawaiians to the year 1950. Including a historical sketch on all the major streets, the major business buildings, its hotels and major historic residences. Photographs of more than 600 buildings, and other items concerning the history of the city of Honolulu." This 643-page typed manuscript (two volumes) is now in the collection of Robert E. Van Dyke.

NOTE: The above is published as a preliminary study. Readers with additions or corrections to this bibliography, or to any other section of this book, are encouraged to write Robert E. Van Dyke at 3059 Maigret Street, Honolulu, Hawaii 96816.

INDEX

Mutual Publishing
2055 North King Street
Honolulu, Hawaii 96819

Produced by Bennett Hymer
Designed by Rubin Young
Reproduction photography by Norman Shapiro
Composition by Alice Matsumoto/Creative Impressions, Honolulu
Text set in 14/17 Colonial Medium, captions set in 10/12 Colonial
Bold. Heads set in 48 point Caslon Openface—all fonts by A/M for
the Compset photo composition machine.

ALA WAI CANAL
UNDER CONSTRUCTION
DIAMOND HEAD   KALAKAUA AVENUE

FUTURE
KEEAUMOKU STREET
AREA

FUTURE
ALA MOANA CENTER

MC

KENNEDY
RESIDENCE

THREE BUILDINGS OF
TERRITORIAL NORMAL SCHOOL

THE NAPOLEAN HOME
SOUTH STREET

PUNCHBOWL STREET

KAWAIAHAO CHURCH

IOLANI PALACE

ALOH
UNDER C
HAWAIIAN ELECTRI
POWER PLANT

ALAPAI STREET

FEDERAL BUILDING

NATIONAL GUARD ARMORY

QUEEN'S HOSPITAL

DOLE PLAYGROUND

CROSS STREET IS PROSPECT STREET

MILL